E.G. Gollner

Gollner's pocket guide of Saratoga Springs

E.G. Gollner

Gollner's pocket guide of Saratoga Springs

ISBN/EAN: 9783337373931

Printed in Europe, USA, Canada, Australia, Japan

Cover: Foto ©Andreas Hilbeck / pixelio.de

More available books at **www.hansebooks.com**

INDEX.

4   INDEX.

HISTORICAL SKETCH.

SARATOGA BATTLE-GROUND.

During the third year of the Revolution, General Burgoyne, with more than ten thousand men, invested Ticonderoga in July, 1777. The small force of only three thousand, under General St. Clair, was obliged to retreat, and the British campaign in the Mohawk valley opened brilliantly. Fear and disaster spread through all the country round about, and the days were dark for the republic. General Schuyler, then in command at Fort Edward, made a call for aid, and the country turned out in great numbers, and the American army quickly rose to thirteen thousand men. General Gates then took command of the new army, and prepared to punish the English. It was in this county that the notable events that followed, took place, and the site of the battles may be seen some fifteen miles north of Saratoga Springs. Burgoyne, with his Indian allies, was obliged to spend four weeks in making the journey to Fort Edward, as the Americans had destroyed all the bridges, and blocked the forest roads with fallen trees. This march will ever remain a lasting shame on the English name. The romantic tragedy of Jane McCrea, the betrothed of a Tory officer, slain by Indians employed by Burgoyne, reflected a strange light on British character, and wrung from Parliament the denunciations such warfare deserved. Little used to such forest fighting, the dainty English army began to wear out its good clothes and fine spirits. It wanted more beef to keep up its courage, and sent over to Bennington to capture Vermont cattle; but Stark was about, and they had a horrible time of it. Before night, another party came for more beef, and unhappily met Colonel Seth Warner with a few Vermont sportsmen and others. More than a thousand hungry Englishmen stopped over in Vermont, or crept into quiet graves, and General Burgoyne lost both beef and men. Naturally, he and his men felt bad, and the pious Indians felt worse still, for they quietly slipped away, and went off into the woods in search of game, and never came back.

Mohawk Indians and the Tories made various kinds of trouble in the Mohawk Valley, but it availed nothing, and after a number of minor encounters, the Americans hushed up matters to the satisfaction of all—save the English. Burgoyne had invited friends to a little Christmas dinner at Albany, but the prospect became doubtful for the guests, and the host looked about in search of some place where he could eat even a lunch in peace. He established a camp at Saratoga, partly on the hills and partly on the plain by the Hudson. The spot is now the village of Schuylerville. General Gates at once advanced to Bemis' Heights, about four miles north of Stillwater, and sat down for a long call. On the 19th of September the two armies met near the British works, and there was a free fight with uncertain results. Burgoyne crept back into his fort, and wondered if anybody would come up from New York to his assistance. Nobody came, and his good Indians and very proper Canadians said they wanted to go home, as it looked just a little squally. The General said they couldn't go—and they all went. Meanwhile, General Gates held a very large party, and a great many fellows called in just to see the fun. Burgoyne and his redcoats, nearly choked with their sixty pounds of baggage and their very stiff cravats, came out to have another little scene. It was a cheerful occasion, and the English army made a very gorgeous show This was on the 7th of October, and that night they all marched back again, feeling pretty bad. The meeting had not been agreeable. More than this, there was no more beef, and Stark hadn't any to sell. Thereupon, General Burgoyne politely made a present of his sword to General Gates on the 17th of October, and the Americans took a fine train of field guns, five thousand muskets, and a vast store of munitions of war. American stock rose twenty per cent. This was Burgoyne's surrender, and one of the great victories of the war.

HISTORY OF SARATOGA SPRINGS.

The name of Saratoga is derived from an old Indian name, *Se-rach-ta-gue,* meaning *the hillside country of the great river,* and referred to that tract of land lying six miles back on either side of the Hudson, and fifteen miles in length, embracing the present townships of Saratoga and Stillwater on the west, and Easton on the east side of the Hudson river. This tract was deeded by the Indians, in 1684, to Peter Philip Schuyler and six other citizens of Albany. It extended, as described in the letters patent, from *Di-on-on-da-ho-wa*, now the Batten Kill, to *Then-en-do-ho-wa*, now the Anthony Kill, near Mechanicsville, on both sides of the *Co-ho-ta-te-a*, now Hudson, river. The tract embracing the present springs was called by the Indians, *Kay-ad-ros-se-ra—the lake country*—and was a favorite hunting ground, the name of which is still retained for the large stream flowing through the county and emptying into the Hudson at Mechanicsville.

When the mineral springs were first discovered by the whites, they unwittingly called them "The Springs near Saratoga," though situated several miles away from the real *Se-rach-ta-gue*, in another hunting ground; and thus the less distinguished robbed the more noted of its name and fame.

> "Ye say they all have passed away,
>   That noble race and brave;
> That their light canoes have vanished
>   From off the crested wave;
> That 'mid the forest where they roamed,
>   There rings no hunter's shout:
> *But their name is on your waters,*
>   *Ye may not wash it out.*"

In the year 1703, one Rip Van Dam and twelve associates took of the Mohawk chiefs an Indian deed of *Kay-ad-ros-se-ra*. It was not until 1768 that the deed, through the powerful influence of Sir William Johnson, was confirmed by the tribe. The chiefs said they were told by the agents of the purchasers that the description in the deed only covered "land enough for a good-sized farm," and that they never intended by it to convey to the whites, "for a few baubles," their great hunting ground containing half a million acres. But after more than sixty years of fruitless quarrels over this old title, the Indians had grown weak and the whites had grown strong, and it is the old story—the weaker gave up to the stronger. In 1770 the tract was surveyed into allotments, and divided among the proprietors and their heirs.   Lot No. 12, of the sixteenth allotment, on which the village of Saratoga Springs now stands, fell to the lot of Rip Van Dam.   He was the first white man who owned the Springs of Saratoga, and he owned them all without even knowing it.

The Indians never having troubled themselves with the trials of getting an education, kept no record of the early history of the Springs at Saratoga.   At least one spring had a prehistoric existence.   The bear, the deer, the wolf and moose were the original patrons of High Rock Spring.   In their eagerness to drink the saline waters, they gathered round this "big salt lick" in great numbers, and were often shot by the Indians while drinking.   The Indians said that the water took away all fear of man, and that the timid deer suffered death rather than forego the salty waters that flowed over the top of the mound-like rock.

The Indians themselves used the waters freely, and regarded the spot as a "medicine spring" that was the direct gift of the Great Spirit for the healing of their nations.   The first white man who visited Saratoga Springs, says Sir William Johnson, was a sick French officer, whom an Indian chief brought from Fort Carillon to be benefited by the waters.   The next, it is believed, was Sir William himself, who came there in August, 1761, ten years before Dirck Scoughten built his pioneer hotel upon the bluff near by.   His faithful Mohawks brought him through the woods from Schenectady, by the way of Ballston Lake, to the High Rock Spring.   Scoughten's route to the springs was from the Hudson to the east side of Saratoga Lake, thence across the lake in a bark canoe to the mouth of the Kayadarosseras River, thence up the river two miles to an Indian trail that led to the springs.   In 1783, General P. Schuyler cut a road through the woods from his mills at the mouth of Fish Creek to the springs, and built a summer-house which he occupied every summer with his family during the rest of his life.

Around those old fountains of *Kay-ad-ros-se-ra*, so often surrounded with the rude wigwams of the savages, the new Saratoga has sprung up in all the pride and splendor of modern civilization.   It has been but a hundred years in building.   In the year 1774 the first rude hotel was opened for the entertainment of visitors by John Arnold, of Rhode Island. He occupied the house built a year or two before by Dirck Scoughten, upon the bluff west of and near High Rock Spring. Scoughten had made a little clearing, planted some potatoes, and put up and partly furnished a log house, when he quarreled with the Indians and they drove him away. This pioneer hotel had but a single room or two on the ground floor, with a chamber overhead. In sight of it were sixteen Indian cabins filled with their savage occupants. In the rocky ledges near by there were numerous dens of rattlesnakes. There were so many of these reptiles then at the springs, that the early visitors often had to hang their beds from the limbs of the trees to avoid them. Nightly the wolves howled and the panther screamed; daily the black bears picked berries in the little clearings, and the wild deer and the moose drank from the brook, while the eagle yearly built her nest in the top of the towering pines.

Such was the style, and such were the surroundings of the first rough hotel of the wilderness springs of a hundred years ago, that led the way in the long line of magnificent structures that have since graced the village.

The individual springs were discovered at various times; some by mere accident, and some by careful scientific search. The oldest of all is the High Rock Spring. It was known to the Indians for a long time before the whites appeared. Its actual age is uncertain, as the Indian accounts of it were mere traditions and legends. The pile of calcareous tufa heaped about the mouth of the spring grew by imperceptible layers, perhaps not an inch in a hundred years, and it is now three and one half feet high, so its age vies with that of the geological period in which we live, and it may be vaguely guessed at thousands of years. For a long time, however, before Sir William's visit, it had ceased to flow over the top, and had found some other outlet. According to an old Indian legend, while it was flowing over the top, some squaws once bathed their sooty faces in it, and the offended waters, shrinking from their polluting touch, sank down in shame into the bosom of the rock, and never afterwards were seen to flow over its surface.

The spring was purchased by Messrs. Ainsworth & McCaffrey in 1865, and in experimenting upon it the firm found that the mound of stone had no connection with the bed rock below. In the black soil below it was found the decayed trunk of a pine, its upper side well worn, as if long-forgotten footsteps had worn it smooth in seeking the spring. Below this were marks of ancient fires, and two distinct layers of tufa and meadow muck, so that the spring may have been in existence long before the present slow-growing rock was formed, and its origin is placed still further back in the total obscurity of prehistoric time. The tubing was finished in August, 1866, and from that time to this the water has flowed out in exhaustless abundance.

Congress Spring was discovered in 1792. In the summer of that year, Governor John Taylor Gilman, of New Hampshire, was staying at the little log tavern that was built by Dirck Scoughten, eight years before, near the High Rock Spring. It was kept by Benjamin Risley, who came from Vermont. Governor Gilman had long been connected with public affairs, and was the popular leader of the Federal party in his native State. He had served with honor in the provincial forces in the war of the Revolution, had been a delegate in the Continental Congress for two years, and was at this time State Treasurer, and from 1794 was, for eleven years, Governor of the State. Upon a pleasant afternoon in August, he took his gun and strolled up the little creek that runs past the High Rock Spring, in search of game. Saratoga was then all a wilderness, excepting a little clearing around the tavern, and two or three others in the vicinity. He followed up the little brook, as it ran through the tangled swamp, until he came to a branch that entered it from the west. This branch then took its rise in a clear spring that ran out of the sand-bank near where the Clarendon Hotel now stands. Running across Broadway, then an Indian trail, a little northerly of the Washington Spring, it emptied into the main brook in what is now Congress street, just below the Congress Spring. A few yards above the mouth of the branch was a little cascade. Below the cascade the rock rose abruptly two or three feet above the level of its bed. Out of this rocky bank, at the foot of the cascade, a little jet of sparkling water, not larger than a pipe stem, spirted and fell into the water of the stream. Struck by its singular appearance, Gilman stopped to examine it. It tasted not unlike the water of High Rock Spring that was already so famous. The truth flashed upon his mind in an instant. He had found a new mineral spring.

Hastening back to his boarding-place, Gilman made known his discovery. Every person in the settlement was soon at the foot of that little cascade in the deep, wild woods, wondering at the curious spectacle. There was Risley and his family, of the Scoughten House; there was Alexander Bryant, the patriot scout of the Revolution, who kept the only rival tavern—a log one, near by Risley's; there was General Schuyler, who had, just ten years before, cut a road through the woods from his mills near the mouth of Fish Creek, to the springs; and Gideon Putnam the founder of the lower village; and Gilman's brother, and a few more guests who were at the little log tavern. And there, too, was Indian Joe, from his clearing on the hill near where the Clarendon now is, and some of his swarthy brethren from their huts near the High Rock, wondering at the strange commotion among the pale faces, at the little waterfall in the brook. And they all, gathering round it, each in turn tasted the water of the newly-found fountain, and pronouncing it of superior quality, they named it, then and there, the Congress Spring, out of compliment to its distinguished discoverer, and in honor of the old Continental Congress, of which he had been a member.

For many years afterwards the water was caught in glasses as it ran from the rock. In attempting to increase its capacity by removing a part of the rock, the spring was lost. But bubbles of gas were noticed in the bed of the creek near by, and, turning the creek one side, excavations were made in its bed. The spring was found and tubed, and has since become world renowned.

Columbian Spring was first tubed, by Gideon Putnam, in 1805. The Ten Springs, near the present Excelsior Spring, were discovered in 1814, and the Washington was tubed in 1806. The Pavilion and Empire Springs were brought into notice in 1836 and 1848. The Geyser group of springs were obtained by boring, and they are comparatively recent. Some of the other springs were known for a long time, but have been only recently developed. So it seems that these remarkable mineral fountains are very old in one sense, and quite new in another. The hidden sources of the waters, and at least one of the escapes at the surface, are very ancient. The tubing and the later boring are comparatively a matter of our own times.

The first critical and scientific examination of the waters was made by Dr. Valentine Seaman, of New York, in 1797 ; and the first large hotel was opened in 1803, by Mr. Gideon Putnam. It was called the Union Hotel, and for a bush hung out a rude picture of " Old Put and the Wolf." The village then consisted of a few log cabins, and the visitors were all invalids. In time, the fame of the cures increased, and the village spread its borders through the wilderness, and began to take on its present rather gorgeous apparel.

Saratoga has, at times, been visited with disastrous conflagrations, which have swept away in an hour some of the magnificent hotels of the town. The first of these, of late date, was in 1865, when the old United States and Marvin Hotels were consumed. They occupied the ground on which the new United States Hotel now stands. The Marvin House was rebuilt on its present site in 1869. The United States was rebuilt in its enlarged and present colossal proportions in 1874, and in June of that year it was opened to summer visitors. The money for building it was raised by the sale of bonds and the enormous sum of $1,000,000 was expended in its construction. The old Congress Hall was destroyed by fire in 1866. The present Congress Hall was built upon the same ground in 1868, at a cost of $800,000, raised by bonds bought by citizens and others, who came forward to assist Mr. Hathorn in repairing the great loss to the town, and replacing it with the present beautiful structure. ·

The Crescent, Park Place and Columbian Hotels, extending from Congress street, on the west side of Broadway, to the grounds of the Clarendon Hotel, were burned, in one conflagration, in the fall of 1871. The Columbian was rebuilt and re-opened in 1872, and the Park Place and Crescent Hotels were replaced, in 1872, by the Grand Hotel, which covered all the ground occupied by the two, with very considerable extensions. The Grand Hotel had a short career, for, on the 1st day of October, 1874, it was obliterated by a sweeping fire that leveled it with the ground. It has not yet been rebuilt, but the vacant lot and ruins on Broadway, corner of Congress street, still perpetuate its memory. The Grand Union has been more fortunate than its rivals, and has gradually assumed its present ornamental and extensive appearance by various enlargements and reconstructions, the last one being the rebuilding of the north wing in the spring of 1875.

Saratoga county was formed from a part of Albany in February, 1791. The first settlements were made by the Dutch, a few years after their arrival in this country. The county, lying on the natural route between the settlements on the Hudson and the French towns in Canada, naturally became the scene of much of the fighting in the early wars between the English and French. After the conquest of Canada, in 1760, the settlements extended rapidly northward, and, by the time of the Revolution, the country had become well filled. During that war, Burgoyne's surrender, and the events that preceded it, made the county famous in our history. The British forces ravaged the entire county, and caused its almost entire depopulation, but the people finally captured the entire English army.

Saratoga Springs, in which we are more particularly interested, was formed from Saratoga township, in 1819, and it was made a post town in 1826. In 1831 a subscription was raised to build a railroad from Schenectady, and it was thought a great thing that the traveler could go to the springs from New York at the the breathless speed of fifteen miles an hour. From that time Saratoga Springs has grown rapidly, and with more or less steadiness. It has had its ups and downs, its fires and hotel openings, its dull times and its periods of wonderful prosperity. To-day it has a permanent population of nine thousand, and offers more attractions than ever. Within the year it has added to its hotel facilities, its social advantages, and its sanitary conveniences. Houses and villas are springing up in its new streets. Better roads and drives are being extended in every direction. Its races and regattas have become established institutions of the pleasure-seeking season. Its springs flow in greater abundance than ever, and in all their abundance there is no decline in their invaluable medical properties. The invalid, the fashionable woman, the idler and the busy city man, may here find, each in their way, something to please and gratify, and none need depart saying that aught is wanting that could contribute to his comfort or happiness.

THE VILLAGE.

The Pictorial Map accompanying this pocket guide is a perfect picture of the village, showing each house in its proper place, and in its proportions. Each public building, church, hotel and spring has a number on its building in the map, corresponding with the index.

In approaching Saratoga Springs over its one railway, either from the north or south, the traveler meets with a surprise. The change from open farms to close-built town is abrupt, and the cars are among the houses and at the station almost before the fields are missed. From the south the first intimation is the little group of cottages clustered about the Geyser Springs, perhaps three minutes before the train stops. From the north the brand-new villas and embryo streets of Excelsior Park, the towers and mansard roofs of the great hotels, flash past just as the brakes begin to pull up for the depot. In either case the train slides along the same covered platform, and "Saratoga" is announced. The intelligent brakeman knows the station is really Saratoga Springs, but, with that freedom for which he is famous, he clips the "Springs." Saratoga is quite another place. This is Saratoga Springs, properly so called. The long platform swarms with importunate hackmen, and were it not for good policing, the arrival would be a trifle formidable. The prudent passenger will provide for the transportation of his baggage, before he reaches the depot, by giving up his checks to the agent of the Saratoga Baggage Express. This company transports baggage to any part of the town for twenty-five or fifty cents, and is a responsible concern. The agent will pass through the cars, just before the train reaches Saratoga, soliciting checks. He can be readily recognized by the badge on his hat, and passengers need have no doubts of his integrity or authority, for none but the reliable agent of the express company is allowed on the cars. By giving him your checks, you will avoid much inconvenience, and have your baggage promptly delivered at your boarding-house without further trouble. To find the porter of your house, a glance at the row of signs overhead will show just where the correct man stands, and where you should go to find him. Each hotel has a reliable man under its sign, and the badge on his hat will make the assurance sure. Give him your checks and then walk to the house. The most distant hotel, except the Mansion House, is only four blocks away, and the little walk will properly introduce one to the place. Unless there are boat or horse-races going on, there is no need to hasten to secure rooms. This is the land of vast hotels, and a party of six or more is a small affair where twenty thousand people may be lodged at once. Opposite the station rise the huge yellow walls of the United States Hotel, and the street beside it leads one to the left, directly upon Broadway, the main thoroughfare of the village. Reaching this street, with the United States on the southern corner (right), and the Arlington Hotel on the northern corner (left), we find ourselves in the centre of the town, on the wide avenue called Broadway. The street is supposed to run up to the north or left, and down to the south or right. The United States, Grand Union, Congress Hall, Columbian, Clarendon and Everett are to the right; the Holden, Waverly, Washington Hall and Broadway Hall are to the left, and each faces the street. The porter will point the way, and each is within ten minutes, excepting the Mansion House at Excelsior Park.

Having found one's house, and a little leisure, it may be in order to look at the village. Saratoga Springs is a village of hotels and dwelling-houses. There are few or no manufactories, and its streets seem devoted to elegant leisure or abundant shopping. Its surface is mainly level, except where a shallow valley winds in a general northeasterly direction through the centre. Through this runs a little brook, and by its banks, at the bottom of the valley, may be found most of the more famous mineral springs. On either side of the valley the ground is level, and forms the top of a piece of elevated table-land, a mile or two in diameter. It is evident that a " fault " occurred here in the geological formation; for, on the west side of this valley, the foundation rock underlying the plateau crops out to the surface, while on the east side, for several feet, nothing but sand is found. The Town Hall, on the corner of Broadway and Lake street, marks the centre of population. The geographical centre is perhaps a quarter of a mile to the southeast of this point.   Immediately beyond the village, and in nearly every direction, the country becomes broken, so that the outskirts are varied and pleasing, while the village itself is sufficiently level for comfortable walking.

The principal street is Broadway, extending a little east of north through the entire village, and making the grand drive and promenade, where all the life, business and pleasure of the place may be seen in a five-minutes' walk.   This concentration of the hotels and stores in one street, and in the immediate neighborhood of nearly all of the springs, gives the village a singular aspect; for, away from this centre, there is nothing but houses, cottages and villas, each, in prim fashion, facing its quiet, shady street—a village of homes.

Broadway is peculiar and original.   The hotels, the elegant stores, the fine rows of trees, the broad borders of sod, and the throng of carriages and people that crowd its walks and roads, present a spectacle unlike anything else in the world.   Newport and Interlaken, Ems and Long Branch, have their special charms, but nowhere else is so much of caravansary and general splendor concentrated in so limited a space.   No other resort can show three such palaces as the United States, to the north, and the Grand Union and Congress Hall, facing each other, on one street.   Perhaps no other place would lug three such monster buildings into such pronounced rivalry.   Be that as it may, here they stand, and the general effect is remarkable and a trifle oppressive.   There is too much of architectural glory; but the American likes grandeur, and here he has it in a profusion perfectly dazzling.   There is a slight bend in the street in the neighborhood of Congress Hall, and standing here, one may look in either direction and feel a natural pride in his country, that such monuments to American wealth, skill and culture can be taken in at a single glance.   Certainly, there is but one Saratoga in the world.

Five minutes' walk, up or down Broadway, takes one past all the great houses and the best stores.   Congress Park and its springs give a rural aspect to the avenue, and the stately rows of trees afford agreeable shade.   The walks are good, and the road well kept. Thousands crowd the way in elegant attire, and there is a world of faces, and things to see and admire. The throng of carriages passes in brilliant procession, flowers and elegant drapery fill the windows and frame the faces looking out, making a bit of realistic fairy-land that wins the attention at every step. The view of the village from the top of the large hotels or the Town Hall is very delightful. The numerous shade trees give the town the appearance of a very beautiful forest city, and the view will fully repay the slight trouble of a few steps to one of these elevations.

Nor are sanitary essentials neglected. With all the paint and varnish, sod-work and gilding, there is no slighting of the unseen works upon which the health and well-being of every town must be built. Excelsior Lake furnishes abundant supplies of pure water, and, by the use of the Holly system of waterworks, it is delivered at every door for domestic and fire purposes. Every street is lighted with gas, and abundant sewers prevent all danger of typhoid visitations.

THE SPRINGS.

The valley in which the springs are found extends in a crescent shape from Ballston Spa to Quaker Springs, a distance of some seventeen miles. The village of Saratoga Springs is located in the very centre of this valley, and includes all the most valuable and the most varied of these natural fountains.

The Source of the Springs.—Geological and scientific people have spent much time in seeking to explain the origin or source of these waters. Rain-water is the usual source of spring-waters. It soaks down through porous soils and rocks, till it meets clay or harder rocks, impervious to fluids. It then, often under great pressure, follows such outlets as it may find, and eventually escapes upward to the surface through some fault or rift in the rocks. On its way it absorbs saline and other mineral substances and gases, and, loaded with them, it reaches the surface, charged in varying proportions, and having a fixed character as mineral water. These proportions do not change materially, and from year to year the waters flow unchanged, and produce on all who drink of them the same general effects.

B

A good authority on the geological aspect reports "that the northern half of Saratoga county is occupied by elevated ranges of Laurentian rocks. The Potsdam, Calciferous, and Trenton beds border upon the Laurentian, and appear in parallel bands through the central part of the county. In the southern part they are covered by slate rocks.

"The Laurentian rocks, consisting of highly crystalline gneiss, granite and syenite, are almost impervious to water, while the overlying Potsdam is very porous, and capable of holding large quantities. The spouting springs and deep wells in the southern part of the county—Geyser, Ballston, etc.—are found in the Potsdam sandstone, which, being covered in these places by the slate rocks and shales, is of great depth."

From the surface downwards the strata are as follows: 1. Hudson River and Utica shales and slates; 2. Trenton limestone; 3. Calciferous sand-rock; 4. Potsdam sandstone; 5. Laurentian formation of unknown depth. Of these the Laurentian alone is impervious to water, and forms the bottom or floor of the cistern which feeds the springs. The dip of the strata is to the south. In the northern part of the county are elevated ranges of Laurentian rock ; thence, going southward, the successive strata crop out parallel to one another, until the village of Saratoga is reached. Here a fault occurs, the rocks being fissured to a great depth, and the strata to the south of the fissure being elevated above the corresponding rocks on the northern side of the cleft. The water percolating through the more porous strata, and finding its way southward along the floor of Laurentian rock, is checked here, and the surplus forced to the surface. The various springs are the outlets of this obstructed water, and their peculiarities and differences are doubtless acquired from the rock and soil through which they reach the surface.

The carbonic acid gas held in the water doubtless aids it in finding an outlet to the surface. Being confined under pressure, it seeks to escape, and brings the water with it. If shut off for a moment, the gas will collect in the top of the pipe wells in such quantities, and and under such pressure, as to blow a steam-whistle. These geological facts have led to the supposition that the waters can be obtained by boring through the slates to the underlying sandstone, and in the case of some of the springs this has proved true, and remarkable supplies have been obtained.

The Temperature of the Water does not vary more than a degree or so in the year, and, in the case of the Congress and Columbian, is 49° Fahr. Other springs are slightly lower or higher, and all are cool and agreeable in warm weather.

The Appearance and Properties of the Water.—When first dipped from the wells the water is limpid and pearly, and full of bubbles. That from the spouting wells gushes forth in creamy whiteness, and resembles soda-water in color and action. The gas quickly escapes, and the still water has a wonderful purity. When allowed to stand open in a glass or uncorked bottle, the transparent water becomes cloudy, a fine white skin forms on the surface, and, in time, a reddish brown precipitate is formed. A glass left empty, and not properly wiped dry, becomes coated with a white film of salts; and around the base of the spouting wells a white incrustation soon forms on the ground, where the spray shivers and spatters on the stones. Left to stagnate on the ground, the water soon becomes covered with a mineral film that shines with metallic lustre and colors, and resembling the tints formed by coal-oils on water. The brook and marsh near the Star Spring show many samples of this curious natural deposit. In cooking, the spring waters are worse than useless.

The first taste of the waters is not always lovely. After the first blush the water becomes exceedingly enjoyable and one is tempted to indulge too freely in the pungent, acidulous and salty mixture. The after-effects resemble those of soda-water, and, if a large quantity is taken, there follows a sense of fullness, perhaps a slight giddiness in the head, and a desire for sleep. These symptoms are only slight, and are soon removed by the discharges that follow; and afterward there comes increased appetite and a feeling of comfortable serenity that is very satisfactory. The various waters, when fresh, have a slightly different taste, and after due experiment one can readily discriminate between them. The iron waters have a slightly inky flavor, and some others leave a sweet taste in the mouth. The gas that bubbles from the surface of the water is fatal to animal life if taken in too large quantities, and it is said that fish cannot live in the water. A whiff of the gas blown in one's face acts as hartshorn, and gives a prickling sensation to the nose. The gas, though suffocating to the lungs when inhaled, is harmless in the water.

Diseases Affected by the Waters.—To give a list in detail would be useless and confusing, and perhaps harmful. There is but one course to pursue in drinking the spring waters for the health's sake. Consult a resident physician, let him make a diagnosis of your case, and under his advice select the particular spring of most value to you, and govern yourself in all things by his experience and acquaintance with the waters. The medical staff of Saratoga Springs is excellent, and one may rely on their ability to assist and direct.

Concerning the directions for their use, much the same thing may be said. As well try to give advice in making prescriptions for the general public. Each user of these healing waters must, in a measure, be a law unto himself. To drink any and all of the waters would be simply unreasonable. Seek proper advice, and then follow it, and be not led aside by the enthusiasm of some invalid who, having been restored to health by some particular spring, thinks it a cure for all diseases, whether they are allied to his special case or not. To persons in perfectly good health, the waters do no particular harm, even if indulged in freely. At the same time, there is reason in all things, and if one is really unwell, there is but one thing to do—consult a medical man.

The late Dr. Steel wrote, in 1837 : "The waters are so generally used, and their effects so seldom injurious, particularly to persons in health, that almost every one who has ever drank of them assumes the prerogative of directing their use to others. Were these directions always the result of careful experience and observation, they would be less objectionable, but there are numerous persons who flock about the springs, without any positive knowledge of the composition and effect of the waters, who contrive to dispose of their directions, many times to the detriment of those who desire to be benefited, but who are thus disappointed in the use of the water."

The Medicinal Action of mineral waters differs in almost every respect from that of cathartics and diuretics, or eliminators in the materia medica. Medicines frequently act by counter-irritation, curing one organ by exciting and irritating another. Ordinary cathartics, diuretics and diaphoretics are composed of substances foreign to the system, and they act partly by their poisonous effects· The most important ingredients of the Saratoga waters are natural to the body, and are also powerful oxydizers of the disintegrated tissues, carrying out of the body the waste matter. Mineral waters are similar to the blood, minus its organic constituents, and are true restorative medicines, as well as powerful modifiers of the tissues themselves ; and these properties, and their gentle mode of action, constitute no small degree of their extraordinary merit.

"Saratoga water is a cholagogue in its properties ; that is, it stimulates the action of the liver, and promotes the excretion of bile. Certain matters are secreted by that organ, which, if allowed to remain in the system, produce such diseases as jaundice. A great number of intestinal diseases and blood disorders are associated with derangements of the functions of the liver.

"The waters are not only laxative or aperient, but are also diuretic, antacid, deobstruent, alterative and tonic.

"They increase the force of the heart and arteries, promote digestion, favor the action of the nutrient vessels, increase the peristaltic movement of the bowels, cleanse the system through the granular organs, and impart strength and vigor."

Congress Spring (3–5 G).—This spring is located in Congress Spring Park, opposite the southern end of Congress Hall. There is an artistic and very beautiful pavilion built over it to protect visitors from the sun and rain. The principal entrance to the spring-house is at the grand entrance to the park, near Broadway. On entering the park, turn to the left, pass along the arbor-like colonnade to the pavilion about the spring, where seats are provided, and the spring water drawn by a novel process, is served upon small tables by the attendants. By descending a few steps to the east, along the colonnade to the *café*, hot coffee and other refreshments may be obtained. Admission to the park is regulated by tickets, for which a merely nominal charge is made, but access to the spring can be obtained on Congress street, without entering the park, and the waters are served free of charge.

Congress Spring was discovered in 1792. The waters were first bottled for exportation in 1823, by Dr. John Clarke, of New York, who purchased the spring from the Livingston family, who held it under an ancient grant. The property was purchased of Dr. Clarke's executors, in 1865, by the Congress and Empire Spring Company, the present proprietors.

The medicinal effects of Congress water have been tested for nearly a century, and its use is prescribed by physicians with the utmost confidence, after long knowledge of its great efficacy, and the entire comfort and safety with which it may be used. To professional men and others whose occupations are sedentary, and to all sufferers from the various forms of bilious disorders, it is invaluable. It contains enough of the laxative salts (chloride of sodium and bicarbonate of magnesia) to render its effects certain without the addition or use of cathartic drugs; and it produces free and copious evacuations without in any manner debilitating the alimentary canal or impairing the digestive powers of the stomach. At the same time it does not contain an excess of those salts, the presence of which in the cruder mineral waters, native and foreign, often renders them drastic and irritating, producing very serious disorders.

Columbian Spring (4-4 G).—This spring is located in Congress Spring Park, just west of the park entrance and on Broadway. It is covered by the beautiful and artistic pavilion, and is approached through the park entrance to the right, or down a few steps from Broadway opposite the Columbian Hotel. The spring is owned by the Congress and Empire Spring Company. It is a fine chalybeate mineral water, and possesses singularly active properties in certain diseases.

It is said to be especially valuable in liver complaints, dyspepsia erysipelas and all cutaneous disorders. As a tonic water for frequent use, no spring in Saratoga is so popular as the Columbian.

The water is recommended to be drank in small quantities frequently during the day, generally *preceded* by the use of the cathartic waters taken before breakfast. Only from one-half to one glass should be taken at a time. When taken in large quantities, or before breakfast, a peculiar headache is experienced.

The proper use of this water will strengthen the tone of the stomach and tend to increase the red particles of the blood, which, according to Liebig, perform an important part in respiration. Though containing but 5.58 grains of iron in each gallon, this water has a perceptible iron taste in each drop. Is it much to be wondered at, then, that a mineral which has so great a power of affecting the palate should possess equally potent influence upon the whole system? The happy medicinal effects of these iron waters seem to consist, to some extent, in the minute division of the mineral properties, so that they are readily taken into the system.

Washington Spring (18-3 G).—The Washington Spring is situated in the grounds of the Clarendon Hotel, on South Broadway. It is a chalybeate or iron spring, having tonic and diuretic properties. It is not a saline water, and the peculiar inky taste of iron is perceptible. It should be drank in the afternoon or evening, before or after meals, or just before retiring.. One glass is sufficient for tonic purposes. Many regard this as the most agreeable beverage in Saratoga. It is frequently called the " Champagne Spring," from its sparkling properties. It is a very popular spring, and in the afternoon is thronged with visitors. Its grounds are very picturesque, and in the evening are lighted by gas.

Crystal Spring (3 G).—This spring has the same general character of the other springs, and is said to be quite as valuable as a medical agent. It is located near the Columbian Hotel, in South Broadway.

Hathorn Spring (9-6 G).—The Hathorn Spring is on Spring street, directly opposite the north wing of Congress Hall. It was discovered, in 1867, by some workmen employed in placing the foundation of the brick block which contains the ball-room of Congress Hall. It is named in honor of the Hon. H. H. Hathorn, who first developed the spring, and built the Congress Hall Hotel. The spring was very securely tubed in 1872. The Hathorn is one of the most valuable springs in Saratoga. Enormous quantities of water are bottled and sold in the leading towns and cities of the United States and Canada.

The water contains 888.03 grains of solid content in a gallon, and combines chloride of sodium, the prevailing chemical element of all the Saratoga spring waters, with bicarbonate of lithia, and other valuable properties.

Hamilton Spring (8-7 H).—The Hamilton Spring is located on Spring street, corner of Putnam street, opposite Hathorn Spring This spring water is equally as good as the majority of the springs of Saratoga, but it has not been taken up by capitalists.

Putnam Spring (13-9 G).—The Putnam Spring is located on Putnam street, one block north of the Hathorn Spring. It is used almost entirely for bathing, for which every facility is provided at the spring.

Pavilion Spring (12-10 G).—The Pavilion Spring is located in the United States Park, between Caroline and Lake avenues, a block and a half east of Broadway. It is surrounded by beautiful shade trees. Though but five feet from the United States Spring, the waters are entirely different in their taste and nature. The pavilion covering this spring is the handsomest in Saratoga.

United States Spring (1-10 G).—This spring is located in United States Park, five feet from Pavilion Spring, though the two springs are entirely different. It is covered with the same handsome pavilion.

Seltzer Spring (15-14 G).—The Seltzer Spring is close to High Rock Spring, and in the neighborhood of the Star and Empire. Although in such close proximity thereto, its water is entirely different, thus illustrating the wonderful extent and capacity of nature's subterranean laboratory. This is the only seltzer spring in this country. The character of the water is almost identical with that of the celebrated Nassau Spring of Germany. The spring pavilion is closed, and its waters are not offered to the public.

High Rock Spring (10-14 G).—The High Rock Spring is on Spring Avenue, near the Empire, Star and Seltzer, and is believed to be the first which was discovered in this vicinity. The peculiar mineral formation which gives it its name is a great curiosity, and early attracted the attention of Indian hunters and the white pioneers of American civilization. The water has built a curb for itself, the foundations of which must have been laid when the continent was in its infancy. The water being impregnated with particles of mineral substances, probably at first saturated the ground about the outlet of the spring. As the water evaporated, a species of rock was formed by the commingling of earth and mineral, and the continual overflow of mineral water gradually built up the present curious, dome-shaped rock, which is three and a half feet high, and twenty-three feet four inches in circumference, and looks like a miniature volcano. There is an Indian tradition that, many years ago, the waters ceased to flow over the rock, owing to the displeasure of the Great Spirit. The water, however, remained within reach from the top, and the overflow probably found a way of escape through cracks which eventually have been stopped by deposits from the water. A handsome pagoda has been erected over the spring, and a bottling-house near by. It is said that the first white man who used these waters was Sir William Johnson, who was brought, in the year 1767, through the wilderness, which then surrounded Saratoga, on a litter, and drank the water a few weeks, when he was able to walk without assistance. The High Rock Spring, which may therefore be looked upon as the father of all these healing waters, has stood the test of over a century. Its water is a superior tonic and cathartic, as well as alterative. It is useful in rheumatism, scrofula, dyspepsia, constipation, and is especially beneficial in its operation upon the kidneys and liver; and indeed, it purifies and renovates the whole system, clearing the complexion and prolonging life. It also cures biliousness, corrects acidity of the stomach, and relieves nervous or feverish irritation and headache.

Saratoga Magnetic Spring (14-16).—The Saratoga Magnetic Spring is situated on Spring avenue, in the valley opposite the High Rock Spring. It is unlike all other springs in Saratoga, having that wonderful magnetic influence which is one of the great marvels of nature. It was discovered recently, but its healing powers and properties have been thoroughly tested, and found to be highly valuable. The waters are not bottled, but are used for bathing purposes. Quite a large number of convenient baths have been built at the spring, and special apartments for ladies have been provided. The baths are found to be highly efficacious in the cure of rheumatism, neuralgia, cutaneous and nervous affections, and have a perceptible tonic influence upon the system. Its valuable qualities are recognized by physicians and residents of Saratoga, and have added another and peculiar feature to this wonderfully rich mineral spring region. All should visit this spring, and while there you may have your knife magnetized by a bath in the spring if you choose. The baths are open from 7 A. M. to 6 P. M. daily, and attendants are at call.

Star Spring (16-15 G).—This spring was formerly known as the President and the Iodine. It is over half a century since its waters were first known and used, but their full virtues were not developed until 1862, when the water was traced to its rocky sources, and the spring tubed in the best manner.

Since then the Saratoga Star Spring has greatly increased its popularity as a mineral water, and is now recognized as one of the leading waters in the principal markets. The water is largely charged with carbonic acid gas, which renders it peculiarly valuable as a bottling water, since it preserves its freshness much longer than waters containing a smaller amount of the gas.

While the immediate effects of the Star Spring are cathartic, its remote effects are alterative, and these, after all, should be considered the most important, as the water thus reaches and changes the morbid condition of the whole system, giving the Star water the high repute which it has maintained from its first discovery. For the following complaints it has been used with marked advantage: scrofula, cutaneous eruptions, bilious affections, rheumatism, gravel, calculus, suppression, fevers, dyspepsia, constipation, diabetes, kidney complaints, loss of appetite and liver difficulties.

Empire Spring (6-16 II).—This spring, one of the best in Saratoga, is located in the north part of the shallow valley that runs through the village. This spring is in a pavilion before the building. For full information concerning this spring, call at the office of the Congress and Empire Spring Company, near Congress Hall. Although the existence of mineral water in this locality was known for a long time, it was not until 1846 that any one thought it worth the necessary expense of excavation and tubing. The rock was struck twelve feet below the surface of the earth, and so copious was the flow of water that the tubing proved to be a work of unusual difficulty. When once accomplished, the water flowed in great abundance and purity. It soon attracted the attention of medical men, and was found to possess curative properties which rendered it available in diseases which had not before been affected by Saratoga waters. It has proved itself adapted to a wide range of cases, especially of a chronic nature, and its peculiar value is recognized by eminent medical men. Its general properties closely resemble the Congress, although, from the presence of a larger quantity of magnesia in the Congress water, the operation of the latter is perhaps somewhat more pungent.

Red Spring (14-16 H).—This spring, so widely and justly celebrated for its curative properties, is located just north of the Empire Spring. It was discovered in 1770, and in 1784 a bath-house was erected at the spring for the cure of eruptive and skin diseases. The efficacy of the water was thereby demonstrated, and since then, though no particular effort has been made to advertise the water, it has become celebrated throughout the entire country. Hundreds of testimonials from eminent people who have used the water both at the original fountain and at their homes, attest its efficacy as a remedial agent. It is a powerful antacid, and is especially adapted to rheumatic and gouty affections. It also neutralizes, by its alkalinity, those acids which produce dyspepsia and its allied diseases. In a general sense, its therapeutic effects are alterative, and it is especially adapted to inflamed mucous surfaces. Scrofula, dyspepsia, kidney difficulties, salt rheum, inflamed eyes, granulated eyelids, are among the diseases which are cured by this water. Its general effect is to tone up the system, regulate the secretions, and vitalize the blood, thereby creating an improved appetite and better assimilation. During the summer season the spring is thronged with invalids. More than a hundred gallons of water are daily taken away by real invalids, besides that which is drank at the spring. The effect of the water, as an alterative, is far superior to that of any other spring, and so great that small quantities produce the desired results, adapting it wonderfully to the weakest stomachs in cases of extreme chronic disease. This quality of the water is due to the peculiar combination of its ingredients. Dr. Steele spoke of the wonderful power of this water in curing salt rheum and skin diseases, fifty years ago, in a work he wrote on the character of "Our Mineral Springs."

The present owners, the Red Spring Company, retubed the spring a few years ago, and erected a spacious bottling-house provided with ample facilities for bottling the water, in order to keep pace with the increasing demand for the water from non-resident patrons.

"A" Spring (1–16 G).—The "A" Spring is situated on Spring avenue, beyond the Empire Spring, and a little north of the Red Spring, on the eastern side of a steep bluff of calciferous sand-rock. It is one of the oldest and best springs in Saratoga. A fine, large bottling-house encloses the spring.

The memory of that reverend being, the oldest inhabitant, does not recall the time when the existence of mineral water in this immediate locality was not known. As the merits of spring waters were so little known and understood in the earlier days of their discovery, no attempt was made to introduce this spring to public attention until 1865, when a shaft twelve feet square was sunk to the depth of sixteen feet, and the spring was first tubed. In the spring of the next year the fountain was more perfectly secured by a new tubing. In 1867 the bottling-house was nearly destroyed by fire, and the spring was again retubed to the depth of thirty-two feet, going down to the solid rock, where one of the most perfect veins of water was found flowing in all its original purity, which was secured with the greatest care, and brought to the surface through a maple tube.

The Saratoga "A" Spring water is one of the most effective mineral waters found on either continent. It has ten per cent. greater mineral properties than the Congress Spring, four times that of Baden Baden of Austria, five times that of Aix-la-Chapelle in Prussia, twice that of the Vichy of France, nearly three times greater than the Seltzer of Germany and equally over the Spas of England and Kissengen in Bavaria.

Minnehaha Spring (11–15 H).—This spring is located a few rods east of the Excelsior Spring.

Excelsior Spring (7–16 H).—The Excelsior Spring is found in a beautiful valley, amid picturesque scenery, about a mile east of the town hall, and near the entrance of Excelsior Park. The principal park entrance is on Lake avenue, half a mile from Circular street, or we may approach it by Spring avenue, which will lead us past most of the principal springs, and the Loughberry Water Works with its famous Holly machinery, by which the village is supplied with an abundance of the purest water from the Excelsior Lake. Leaving the water works, we see just before us, as the avenue bends towards the Excelsior Spring, the fine summer hotel known as the Mansion House. Surrounded by its grand old trees and beautiful lawn, it offers an inviting retreat from the heat and dust of our crowded cities.

The spring is covered by a very tasteful pavilion, which will be noticed just east of the little stream, and in front of the large bottling-house beside the grove. The Union Spring is a little northwest of the Excelsior, and but a few steps removed. This valley in which these two springs are situated was formerly known as the " Valley of the Ten Springs," but the present owners, after grading and greatly beautifying the grounds, changed its name in honor of the spring to Excelsior Park.

The tubing of the Excelsior Spring extends to a depth of fifty-six feet, eleven of which are in the solid rock. By this improvement the water flows with all its properties undeteriorated, retaining from source to outlet its original purity and strength.

Brook Spring (2-16 G).—The Brook Spring is located in Excelsior Park, near Excelsior Spring.

Union Spring (17-16 H).—The Union Spring, near the centre of Excelsior Park, is about ten rods northwest of Excelsior Spring. It was originally known as the Jackson Spring. The water was, however, but imperfectly secured until the present proprietors had the spring retubed in 1868. The water of the Union Spring acts as a mild cathartic when taken before breakfast. Drank at other times during the day, it is a very agreeable and healthful beverage.

Eureka White Sulphur Spring.—This valuable spring is situated about a mile east of the village, and about a quarter of a mile east of the Excelsior Spring. It should not be confounded with the sulphur spring on the east side of Saratoga Lake, some ten miles from the village. The water of this spring is used for bathing and drinking, and is bottled by a process by which all the medical and curative properties of the water are preserved. The curative properties of it are fully established, and there is a large and very commodious bathing-house, containing fifty baths, and supplied with every convenience for giving warm or cold sulphur baths at all hours of the day. This spring supplies a very important element to the attractions of Saratoga. The other springs supply valuable mineral waters to be taken internally, while the White Sulphur waters supply that very important element of medicinal effects produced by bathing. Persons afflicted with rheumatism or cutaneous diseases always receive positive benefit, and generally are completely cured by using these baths. The water is very pure, containing no mineral matter whatever except sulphur. Male and female attendants are always at hand during bathing hours, and every convenience for luxurious and wholesome bathing is afforded.

The trains of the Saratoga Lake Railway Company run at short intervals from the village to the bath-house. Fare each way, only five cents, in elegant and commodious cars.

Eureka Spring.—A few yards south of the White Sulphur Spring is the mineral Eureka Spring. Its water is highly charged with carbonic acid gas, making it one of the most pleasant to the taste of all the Saratoga waters. It is a superior tonic, diuretic and mild cathartic.

Diamond Spring.—The Diamond Spring is just north of the Vichy, in its grounds, and is a valuable chalybeate or iron spring, with ingredients quite unlike those of its near neighbors. It possesses valuable tonic and diuretic properties, and is specially recommended for those suffering from general debility. One glass has the exhilarating effect of champagne, and it is remarkably efficient in curing many complaints peculiar to the female sex. It contains a large amount of carbonic acid gas, and bottles better than any iron water at Saratoga.

Geyser Spring.—The Geyser or Spouting Spring is a most wonderful fountain of mineral water, discovered in 1870, and situated about a mile and a quarter southwest of the village, in the midst of the beautiful region of landscape scenery known as Geyser Lake and Park. To reach it from Saratoga, follow Broadway south to

Ballston avenue, which branches off from Broadway in the southern part of the village to the right, towards the southwest, and follow this avenue until it crosses the Renssalaer and Saratoga Railroad, when the large brick bottling-house, with the inscription of "Geyser Spring," will be distinctly seen across the lake to the left. Follow the carriage road across the causeway turning to the left, and you will soon find yourself at the entrance of the spring and bottling-house, and in the midst of the most interesting spring region of Saratoga Visitors are most cordially welcomed to the spring and grounds by the owners of the property, Settle & Cary, and perfect freedom is accorded to all visitors to drink the waters, inspect the work of bottling, and to stroll through the beautiful grounds surrounding the springs. As you enter the spring-house, directly in front of you in the centre of the building, is this marvelous spouting spring, sending forth a powerful stream of water to the very top of the building, which, in descending to its surrounding basin, sprays into a thousand crystal streams, forming a beautiful fountain, ever flowing, and charming to behold.

The orifice bored in the rock is five and a half inches in diameter and one hundred and thirty-two feet deep. The rock formation consists of a stratum of slate eighty feet thick, beneath which lies the stratum of birdseye limestone in which the mineral vein was struck. The orifice is tubed with a block-tin pipe, encased with iron, to the depth of eighty-five feet, the object being to bring the water through the soft slate formation, as the immense pressure and force of the gas would cut the slate, thereby causing impurities in the water. Before leaving the house, record your name in the visitors' register on the desk to the right of the entrance. On this register are the names of over one hundred thousand visitors who visited the spring in the past season, thus attesting to the great popularity of this interesting phenomenon. Twenty-seven omnibuses are employed daily in the season in bringing visitors from the village to this celebrated spring.

Champion Spouting Spring.—This phenomenal fountain is about a mile and a half south of the village of Saratoga Springs, near the carriage road leading to Ballston Spa, just east of the railroad. It is one of the group of celebrated spouting springs which have recently been developed and become a wonderful feature of the great watering place. It was discovered in 1871, after sinking a shaft to the unusual depth of three hundred feet. From this deeply-concealed cavern the precious fountain burst forth to light, sending a column of water six and a half inches in diameter, twenty-five or thirty feet into the air, presenting a marvelous and beautiful spectacle. The gaseous force of the water has been checked by a strong iron cap, fastened to the top of the tubing, and only a small jet of water is allowed to escape, except at five o'clock in the afternoon, when this cap is removed, and the water darts forth in large volume to a height of eighty to a hundred feet, imitating the wonderful Yellowstone and Iceland Geysers. These Saratoga Geysers are exceedingly interesting, and should be visited. During the winter the water freezes around the tube, and gradually forms a column of solid ice from thirty to forty feet high, and several feet in diameter. This marvelous spring possesses the chemical elements common to the Saratoga spring waters in larger quantities than any other spring yet developed.

It contains more mineral properties per gallon than any other spring water in Saratoga. Hence, a less quantity will produce the usual effect. It acts very favorably upon the kidneys and liver, and its medicinal value is established by the testimony of high medical authority.

Kissengen Spring.—The Kissengen Spring is a pipe well, one hundred and seventy-two feet deep, on the east side of the Geyser Lake.

Packing the Waters for Domestic and Export Transportation.—The bottling and packing is carried on throughout the year, and, except during the height of the visiting season, when so much is consumed at the springs as materially to decrease the supply for bottling, the work is prosecuted night and day. The arrangements for this purpose are the most complete of anything of the kind in the country, and all the various operations are carried on with a care, skill and perfection unsurpassed.

In order to increase the facilities for obtaining bottles, the Congress and Empire Spring Company erected a good glass-house some time since, and now, not only this company, but many of the others, are easily supplied with such bottles as they need. Some of the bottles are of dark glass, and others, like those used by the Geyser Company, are of white or crystal glass.

The bottles are securely packed in wooden boxes, and every box is fully marked to prevent all mistake. Each box contains a con-. venient quantity for family use, which is usually two dozen quart or four dozen pint bottles.

The waters are either pumped through block-tin pipes from the springs, or the water is forced into the bottles by its own hydrostatic pressure. When pumps are employed, a large receiver is used to hold the water under pressure and free from contact with the air, and in drawing it the utmost care is taken to prevent the escape of the gas held in the water. In the case of the pipe wells, the water is drawn like so much soda-water into the bottles from pipes that tap the main wells many feet below their outlets.

The corks, after being soaked in warm water until they become so soft as to be easily compressed, are driven into the bottles by machinery, the process reducing their size before entering the bottles about one-third. It requires a strong bottle to stand the pressure of their expansion after being driven in, and even strong men sometimes find it difficult to pull them out. A single workman will fill and cork from fifteen to twenty dozen bottles per hour.

When the bottles and corks have been thoroughly tested, the corks are securely wired, this operation being performed with great rapidity by employees long trained to the work.

The proprietors of the springs are always pleased to show the wonders of their bottling plants to visitors, and an instructive hour may well be spent in them.

The rows of men and boys, bare-armed before the steaming washing tubs; the salt-encrusted receivers, and the bottle-filler with dextrous fingers loading up the pints and quarts; the corker, with his queer machinery; the huge bins of full or empty bottles, piled in countless thousands, one over the other; the curious industry of the wire-boys and packers, and the vast caverns of the storage cellars, all unite to make a scene of singular interest, and the intelligent visitor should make it a point to see at least one of these immense establishments.

C

The export of spring water in casks is somewhat different. The casks are of the best of oak, and are securely lined with pure block-tin.

There are two openings in these casks at the top, and to each is secured a block-tin pipe. One pipe extends nearly to the bottom of the cask, and the other is only an inch or two long. In filling the cask the water pipe from the spring is screwed to the top of the larger pipe, and the water, under the pressure of its gas, flows in and, driving the air out of a small air-hole, fills the cask. When it is full, the air-hole is stopped up, but the pressure is continued for a moment or two longer, so that the cask is not only filled solidly, but is packed, so to speak, and the water is under the same pressure in the cask as in its native spring. In these casks the waters of the Excelsior, Geyser and other springs are readily transported to all parts of the country. In drawing the water, a block-tin pipe, with a suitable cooler, is attached to the longer pipe, and a small air-pump to the shorter pipe. On pumping air into the cask, the water flows out through an ordinary soda-fountain faucet in its native purity. When the casks are empty they are returned for refilling, and it often happens that a single dealer will have two or more casks constantly on the road, going and coming each way, perhaps two thousand miles or more by rail or boat.

The Danger of Manufactured Mineral Waters.—The value and importance of Saratoga's waters, and the ever-growing demand for them has stimulated the manufacture of artificial waters. Owners of soda apparatus, and druggists with small knowledge and smaller consciences, have concocted a number of queer mixtures that they call mineral waters. Some of these strange drinks are about as useful and harmless as good Croton water, and vastly dearer, for one can have that for the asking. Some are put up in bottles and siphons, and called after famous Saratoga springs, and are even packed in abandoned Saratoga cases. Their only connection with Saratoga is in name, and the name is a fraud and a pretence. Even the trade-marks of the springs have been imitated.

MEDICAL INSTITUTIONS.

The institutions for the special treatment of diseases in Saratoga are few, but one or two are recognized by the medical fraternity as quite superior, and are certainly well supplied with medical appliances, and are under competent management.

Dr. Strong's Remedial Institute (88–9 J).—This institution is situated on Circular street, the most beautiful avenue in Saratoga, only a short distance from the great hotels and one block from the Congress Park.

It is conducted in summer with especial reference to the accommodation of summer boarders, and enjoys a most excellent reputation for its superior advantages as a summer resort. The table is excellent, and the rooms are large, well ventilated, and kept with especial reference to health, as well as comfort and luxury. In summer no one would suppose it to be a medical institute from its appearance, and yet there may be enjoyed the most luxurious baths and means of physical exercise which every summer resort should supply, but which so few, even of the hotels and boarding-houses in Saratoga, afford within their doors.

The institution is supplied with new and the most improved appliances now known to medical science, among which are the Electro-Thermal, Sulphur, Vapor, Turkish and Russian Baths, Swedish Movement Cure, the Equalizer or Vacuum Treatment, Inhalations of Oxygen, also of Compressed and Rarified Air, Gymnastics, and other varieties of Hydropathy and medicine. The whole institution, with its treatment, is supervised by Drs. Sylvester S. and Sylvester E. Strong, regular physicians, graduated at the medical department of the University of New York, and is open all the year.

Dr. Robert Hamilton's Medical Institute (4 C).—This institution, on Franklin street, is established for the treatment of various chronic and special diseases. Many are familiar with his institution that stood on the corner of Broadway and Congress street. It was burned in the disastrous fire that swept away the Park Place and Crescent Hotels. In the spring of 1874, Dr. Hamilton opened his institute on Franklin street, where he receives patients and guests throughout the year.

The institution is kept open as a summer boarding-house during the season, and is kept in good style and in such a manner that no features of a medical institute are observable, and all the medical patrons will be most conscientiously and ably treated, and the pleasure guests cared for with faithful attendance to their wants.

Eureka White Sulphur Spring.—This valuable spring is situated about a mile east of the village, and about a quarter of a mile east of the Excelsior Spring. It should not be confounded with the sulphur spring on the east side of Saratoga Lake, some ten miles from the village. The water of this spring is used for bathing and drinking, and is bottled by a process by which all the medical and curative properties of the water are preserved. The curative properties of it are fully established, and there is a large and very commodious bathing-house, containing fifty baths, and supplied with every convenience for giving warm or cold sulphur baths at all hours of the day. This spring supplies a very important element to the attractions of Saratoga. The other springs supply valuable mineral waters to be taken internally, while the White Sulphur waters supply that very important element of medicinal effects produced by bathing. Persons afflicted with rheumatism or cutaneous diseases always receive positive benefit, and generally are completely cured by using these baths. The water is very pure, containing no mineral matter whatever except sulphur. Male and female attendants are always at hand during bathing hours, and every convenience for luxurious and wholesome bathing is afforded.

The trains of the Saratoga Lake Railway Company run at short intervals from the village to the bath-house. Fare each way, only five cents, in elegant and commodious cars.

CHURCHES.

The churches of Saratoga Springs are commodious and elegant, and designed for the accommodation of both transient and permanent residents. The regular pastors are men of ability and worth, and the various pulpits are often filled during the summer season by eminent divines from all parts of the country.

Baptist Church (75–5 E).—The Baptist Church is located on Washington street, near Grand Union Hotel.

Methodist Church (77–5 E).—The Methodist Church, a handsome structure of brick with sandstone trimmings, is on the north side of Washington street, near Grand Union Hotel.

Episcopal Church (76–5 E).—The Episcopal Church is on Washington street, and directly in the rear of the Grand Union Hotel.

Roman Catholic Church (80–3 G).—This church is located on South Broadway, corner of William street, and opposite the Windsor Hotel.

Presbyterian Church (79–10 F).—The Presbyterian Church is a large brick building with a tall spire, and is next below the town hall, on Broadway.

Congregational Church (75–7 G).—The Congregational Church is on Phila street, second building from Broadway.

Second Presbyterian Church (81–2 A).—This church occupies Newland Chapel, on Spring street.

Free Methodist Chapel (82–7 J).—This chapel is on Regent street, near Union avenue.

Temple Grove Seminary (100 S J).—The Temple Grove Seminary is on Spring street, opposite Indian encampment, three blocks east of Broadway.

The Saratoga daily paper will give in the Saturday edition the hour of service and the names of the pastors.

PUBLIC INSTITUTIONS.

Saratoga is well prepared to accommodate her guests in regard to public institutions and enterprises.

Post Office (90–7 F).—The post office is in the Arcade, on the east side of Broadway, between the Grand Union and the United States Hotels, on the opposite side.

Railroad Depot (91–6, 7, D).—The railroad depot is located one block west of Broadway, on Division street.

Express Office (92–7 D).—The express office is annexed to the railroad depot.

Town Hall (101–9, 10, F).—This building is occupied by the town offices and by the Young Men's Christian Association, and is quite an architectural structure with its high tower and clock, which furnishes the village with correct time.

Congress Park (85-3, 4, 5, 6, G, H, I).—Congress Park is located in the heart of the village, with its immediate neighborhood, fronting the Grand Union, Congress Hall, Columbi n, Clarendon and Windsor Hotels. The Columbian and Congress Springs are within its grounds. The park is laid out in a highly artistic manner. It has a small lake in the centre, and its trees afford the visitor a pleasant and shady retreat.

HOW TO REACH IT.

The village of Saratoga Springs, with its various natural mineral springs, is in the State of New York, U. S. A., one hundred and eighty-two miles north of New York city, and two hundred and thirty miles west of Boston. It is known all around the globe as one of the most fashionable of summer resorts, and it can be reached in through palace cars from New York, Boston, Chicago, &c., during the season, and also by steamers on the Hudson from New York, via Albany or Troy, which will afford the tourist a view of some of the most magnificent scenery in the world.

From New York.—Grand Central Depot, New York Central and Hudson River Railroad to Albany, then by Delaware and Hudson Canal Company's railroad, Saratoga division, to Saratoga. Through palace cars running during the season. There are three lines of steamboats, each having magnificent palace steamers.

The Day Line of steamers from Pier 39, North River, New York, at 8 30 A. M., and from West Twenty-second street at 9 A. M., offers the most magnificent scenery on the Hudson from New York to Albany, from there by daylight, via Delaware and Hudson Canal Company's railroad to Saratoga.

People's Evening Line, from Pier 41, North River, foot of Canal street, New York, at 6 P. M. The palatial steamers "St. John," Capt. Thos. Post, (Monday, Wednesday and Saturday,) and "Drew," Capt. J. S. Roe, (Tuesday, Thursday and Saturday,) connecting with the Delaware and Hudson Canal Company's railroad, at Albany, by daybreak.

Citizens' Evening Line of steamers from Pier 44, North River, foot of Christopher street, at 6 P. M., daily except Saturday, on the Hudson, for Troy, N. Y., connecting with the Delaware and Hudson Canal Company's railroad, by early train, for Saratoga.

From Philadelphia.—To New York by the shortest route, and then by steamer or rail to Saratoga.

From Baltimore.—To New York, and then by steamer or rail to Saratoga.

From Washington.—To New York, and then by steamer or rail to Saratoga.

From the Southeast.—To New York, and then by steamer or rail to Saratoga.

From Boston.—Hoosac Tunnel route (Fitchburg, Troy and Greenfield Railroad, Hoosac Tunnel, and Troy and Boston Railroad,) to Troy, N. Y., then by Delaware and Hudson Canal Company's railroad, Saratoga division, to Saratoga. Passengers can, if they prefer, diverge at Fitchburg, Mass., via Cheshire Railroad, to Bellows Falls, Vt., and then by Rutland division of Central Vermont Railroad to Saratoga.

Or by Boston and Albany Railroad to Springfield, Mass., and Albany, N. Y., and thence, via Delaware and Hudson Canal Company's railroad, to Saratoga. Passengers by this route can, if they prefer, diverge at South Framingham, Mass., and thence proceed, via Boston, Clinton, Fitchburg and New Bedford Railroad, to Fitchburg. Palace cars are run without change from Boston to Saratoga on all these lines.

From Maine and the maritime provinces, rail or boat may be taken to Boston or to Portland. From Portland the Boston and Maine Railroad connects with Manchester, N. H., and then, via Concord and Northern Railroad, to White River Junction, Vt., thence, via Bellows Falls and Rutland, to Saratoga. Or from White River Junction take Central Vermont Railroad to Burlington Vt., thence, by steamer on Lake Champlain or Central Vermont Railroad, to Ticonderoga, N. Y., thence by Delaware and Hudson Canal Company's railroad to Saratoga; or on from Burlington, via Central Vermont, to Rutland, and thence by Delaware and Hudson Canal Company's railroad to Saratoga. Or from Portland, Me., take Portland and Ogdensburg Railroad to White Mountains, St. Johnsbury, Vt., Cambridge and Burlington, and thence by rail or steamer, as above.

From the White Mountains a through palace car is run to Saratoga in one day, in summer, via the Wells River and Montpelier Railroad, Central Vermont Railroad, and Delaware and Hudson, Canal Company's railroad, via Wells River, Montpelier, Burlington, Leicester Junction, Ticonderoga and Whitehall, to Saratoga.   •

Or by Portland and Ogdensburg Railroad from White Mountains to Cambridge and Burlington, Vt., thence by rail or steamer.

From Montreal the most direct route is by the Delaware and Hudson Canal Company's line to Rouse's Point, and thence to Saratoga. Palace cars are run through from Montreal to Saratoga and New York.

Another route from Montreal is via the Grand Trunk Railroad to St. John's, thence via Central Vermont to Rutland, where you change cars; thence, via Delaware and Hudson Canal Company's railroad, to Saratoga.

Or by Grand Trunk Railroad to Rouse's Point, Lake Champlain steamers to Ticonderoga, and thence by Delaware and Hudson Canal Company's railroad, to Saratoga Springs. The latter route is the more delightful, as it takes the tourist through the glorious scenery of Lake Champlain, on the fine steamers of the lake, and also allows a divergence at Ticonderoga, via Lake George.

From Chicago.—Via Buffalo, Niagara Falls and Albany, to Saratoga.

From Cincinnati.—Via Buffalo and Albany, to Saratoga.

From San Francisco and the Far West.—Via Chicago, Niagara Falls and Albany, to Saratoga.

From St. Louis.—Via Indianapolis, Buffalo and Albany, to Saratoga. By taking the Chicago route, the tourist can also visit Niagara Falls. Proceed thence via Albany.

From New Orleans.—By steamers on the Mississippi to St. Louis, affording the tourist some delightful scenery. From St. Louis the most interesting route is by Chicago and Niagara Falls.

Or from New Orleans to Cincinnati, and thence, via Buffalo and Albany, to Saratoga.

From the Southwest and Mexico.—By rail to St. Louis, Chicago, Niagara Falls and Albany, to Saratoga. Or by coastwise steamers to New York, and thence by rail or boat to Albany and Saratoga.

From Europe.—Tourists usually choose New York as the starting-place for Saratoga, as the route includes the Hudson river, giving a choice of boat or rail; the water route giving one hundred and forty-four miles of steamboat voyage of interesting beauty and grandeur, unsurpassed by any other river in the world.

HOTELS AND THEIR FACILITIES.

The hotels at Saratoga Springs are among the largest, the most costly, elegant and comfortable in the world. For nearly a century, people have journeyed to these springs, to drink their healing waters; and, as one day's visit is hardly worth the while, they have sought a home here during the summer season. It is this that has caused the village to open its doors so freely, and to build up, from a small beginning, a system of hotels and boarding-houses unlike anything else to be found. Added to this came, in time, the demands of the merely pleasure-seeking, fashionable world. People came to the springs for the sake of the gay company gathered here, and from year to year the hotels have grown, expanding their wings and adding room beyond room, till they cover acres of ground, and the halls and piazzas stretch out into miles. They have a bewildering fashion here of repeating the wondrous tale of these things. They talk about the miles of carpeting, the thousands upon thousands of doors and windows, the hundreds of miles of telegraph wires, vast acres of marble floors, and tons of eatables stored in the pantries, till one is lost in admirable confusion. It is all true, and that is the wonder of it. The management that governs it all is more remarkable than the gilding and mirrors. It is a sort of high science, unequaled in the world, combining the "ease of mine inn" and a perfection of detail and freedom from friction that is as pleasant as it is wonderful.

Saratoga's face is her fortune, and it is said that the entire town devotes its days and nights to the comfort of the tourist. The tourist should be indeed happy.   If he is not, it is safe to say it is his own fault.

Grand Union Hotel (34-3 to 6·E, F, G).—This palatial hotel occupies almost the entire square bounded by Broadway, Congress, Federal and Washington streets, in the very centre of the town.   It is a magnificent structure of brick and iron, of modern style, with a street frontage of two thousand four hundred feet.   It is undoubtedly the largest and most elegantly furnished water-place hotel in the world.   Along its entire Broadway front of eight hundred feet runs a graceful iron piazza three stories high, affording a splendid promenade which overlooks the liveliest portion of Broadway and the beautiful Congress Park and Spring.   The interior arrangements of this hotel are unsurpassed for completeness, convenience and elegance by any watering-place hotel in the world.   The main entrance and office are at the centre of the Broadway front, in the rotunda, which is eighty feet in diameter, and extends to the top of the house, with balconies on each of the five stories, overlooking the entrance and grand saloon about the office.   To the left of the office are reception-rooms and the grand saloon-parlor, the most beautifully decorated and handsomely-furnished drawing-room in the world, and in the summer evenings, during the season, presents the most brilliant scene of watering-place festivities to be found.

Passing through the drawing-room, we find other smaller private parlors; and turning to the right, into the Congress street wing, we enter the spacious and elegant dining-hall, sixty feet wide, two hundred and seventy-five feet long, beautifully frescoed, and furnished with splendid mirrors, which reflect the festal scene, and add lustre to the brilliant assemblies which congregate in this sumptuous dining-hall.   The dining-room has been lengthened seventy-five feet, and a new fire-proof kitchen and serving-rooms added, and the ventilation of the whole cuisine department made the most perfect possible.   The dining-hall and its appurtenances are now undoubtedly the finest and most complete in the world.

The rooms of the hotel are elegantly furnished, and many are arranged in suites for family use, handsomely frescoed, and supplied with pure, fresh, running spring-water, hot and cold, in every room. Three elevators are now in operation, and guests are conveyed to and from the five floors with the utmost ease and despatch. The hotel fronts on three streets, thus affording a large number of out-side rooms, while the rear rooms open upon the handsome interior court-square, beautifully adorned with trees, shrubs and flowers, presenting a delightful view of genuine artistic landscape garden-ing. On three sides of this court is a wide promenade piazza, which affords a delightful retreat, and yet commands a scene of entrancing beauty. The interior grounds have been greatly beautified and en-larged by the removal of the Opera House and adjacent buildings, and the extension of new walks and retreats to Federal and Wash-ington streets. Its grounds are the largest connected with any hotel in Saratoga, and the magnificent elms afford delightful shade during the summer days of the season.

The new ball-room, sixty by eighty-five feet, built in 1876, is most beautifully proportioned and frescoed, and adorned with bal-conies of the most attractive character. Yvon's Grand Centennial Picture, "The Genius of America," painted expressly for the late Mr. Stewart, occupies one entire end of the room. The assemblies in this beautiful hall are unexcelled in brilliancy by any similar entertainments in the country. The music is supplied by an ex-cellent band of artistic performers, and concerts are given every morning on the piazzas of the hotel, and hops every evening in the ball-room. Entertainments for the children, under the direction of competent professors, are held every week. Garden parties and summer-night "Fête Champétres" are given frequently during the season, and a "German" once each week. No effort or expense is spared by the managers to secure the highest enjoyment possible to the guests of the Grand Union at these entertainments.

Billiard-tables and new bowling-alleys are provided for the ex-clusive use of guests, and all facilities that can conduce to comfort and entertainment are provided by the liberal management of this palatial hotel.

Its past management has secured for it a most enviable reputa-tion ; but Mr. Henry Clair, the present lessee, will accommodate two thousand guests.

United States Hotel (43-5 to 7, D, E, F).—This magnificent structure was completed in June, 1874, and is situated on the block bounded by Broadway and Division street, on the site of the old United States Hotel, around which so many pleasant memories cluster, but which was burned a few years ago. It constitutes one continuous line of buildings, six stories high, over fifteen hundred feet in length, containing nine hundred and seventeen rooms for guests, and is the largest hotel in the world. The architectural appearance is exceedingly elegant and beautiful. It is Norman in style, and its mansard roof is embellished with pediments, gables, dormer windows and crestings, and three large pavilions.

The building covers and encloses seven acres of ground, in the form of an irregular pentagon, having a frontage of two hundred and thirty-two feet on Broadway, six hundred and fifty-six feet on Division street, with "Cottage Wing" on the south side of the plaza, extending west from the main front for five hundred and sixty-six feet. This wing is one of the most desirable features of this admirably-arranged house, as it affords families and other parties the same quiet and seclusion which a private cottage would afford, together with the attention and conveniences of a first-class hotel. The rooms of this wing are arranged in suites of one to seven bedrooms, with parlor, bath-room and water-closet in each suite. Private table is afforded, if desired, and the seclusion and freedom of a private villa may be enjoyed here, to be varied, at will, by the gayer life of the hotel and watering-place.

The main front and entrance is on Broadway, in which is the elegant drawing-room, superbly furnished with Axminster carpets, carved walnut and marble furniture, frescoed ceilings, elegant lace curtains, and costly chandeliers and mirrors. The room is rich and tasteful in its entire arrangements. Across the hall is the ladies' parlor, furnished with exquisite taste; and beyond, at the corner of the Broadway and Division street fronts, are the gentlemen's reading-rooms and the business offices of the hotel. To the west of the office in the Division street wing, is the dining-hall, fifty-two by two hundred and twelve feet, with twenty and one-half feet ceiling; beyond which are the private drawing-rooms, the children's ordinary, carving-rooms, etc. The grand ball-room, one hundred and twelve by fifty-three feet, with ceiling twenty-six feet high, is on the second floor of the Division street wing, and is decorated with artistic and appropriate adornments. The arrangement of the sleeping apartments of this hotel is excellent, and its rooms are furnished with gas, water and marble basins throughout, and has running water in all its rooms. All the rooms are connected with the office by an electric annunciator. The entire building is divided into five sections by thick, fire-proof walls, and the openings through them are protected by heavy iron doors, thus affording great protection in case of fire. There are also fire-hydrants in each section, with hose attached, on each floor. There are ten staircases, which afford ample means of escape from fire. Two elevators are used solely for conveying guests to the various floors, and every convenience has been adopted in equipping this elegant hotel for its immense summer business. Upon the Broadway front is a fine piazza, two hundred and thirty-two feet long, three stories high, overlooking the centre of the village; and one on Division street, two hundred feet in length. Extensive piazzas, two thousand three hundred feet in length, for promenades, encircle the large interior court, which is ornamented with beautiful shade trees, sparkling fountains, graceful lawn-statuary and meandering walks; and, during the evening, when illuminated with colored lights and lanterns, and enlivened with exquisite music, the scene is brilliant and fascinating in the extreme.

This immense and elegant hotel is managed by gentlemen of great experience. The Hon. James M. Marvin, who is well known to all old frequenters of Saratoga, has the general control of the whole interest, while Messrs. Tompkins, Perry, Gage and Janvrin are the lessees and proprietors. Will accommodate two thousand guests.

Congress Hall (28–5, 6, G).—Congress Hall is built on the site of the old and famous hotel of the same name, which was burned in 1866, and occupies the larger part of the square bounded by Broadway, East Congress, Spring and Putnam streets. Its situation is in the very centre of the gay and fashionable hotel world of Saratoga, and is admirably arranged for seeing all the attractive phases of the "great watering-place life." Its frontage on Broadway, the principal street of the town, is four hundred and sixteen feet, with a high promenade piazza twenty feet wide and two hundred and forty-nine feet in length, commanding a view of the most brilliant portion of Saratoga. From the Broadway front two immense wings, three hundred feet long, extend to Putnam street, the northern wing, running along Spring street and overlooking the celebrated Hathorn and Hamilton Springs on one side, and with the central wing, which runs parallel with it, enclosing a very beautiful garden-plot. The southern front commands a full view of the famous Congress and Columbian Springs, and the beautiful Congress Park. Ample piazzas extend around the back of the hotel, overlooking the grass and garden-plots of the interior court, affording cool and shady retreats in the afternoon, when entrancing music is discoursed.

Congress Hall was purchased in 1878 by Mr. W. H. Clement, of Cincinnati, Ohio, and Mr. John Cox, of New York, who have placed it under permanent management.

Congress Hall is built of brick, with brown-stone trimmings. The roof is a mansard, with three pavilions, which affords wide and delightful views from the promenades on top. Interior fire-walls are provided to prevent the spread of fire, and Otis elevators afford easy access to all the floors of the house. The rooms are all large, high and well ventilated, and properly provided with annunciators, gas, etc. The halls, dining-rooms, parlors and offices are of grand proportions, and are furnished with an elegance that bespeaks comfort and neatness in all its departments. The ventilation of the dining-room and kitchen has been much improved, and a steam heating apparatus introduced on the main floor for use whenever changes in the temperature require it. Hot and cold water have been carried to every floor, and a large number of baths and closets added for the convenience of guests. The ball-room of the Congress is one of the finest in Northern New York, being most exquisitely frescoed and adorned with costly chandeliers and ornaments. It is in the block across Spring street, but is connected with the north wing of the hotel by a light, graceful iron bridge suspended over the street, properly covered and protected, which, when illuminated on hop nights, is very picturesque. Will accommodate fifteen hundred guests.

Clarendon Hotel (25-3, F, G).—This Hotel is located on

Broadway, a short distance south of the Grand Union Hotel, and opposite the Windsor, with one of the pleasantest sights in the village. It partly encloses within its wings a depression or valley, ornamented with shady trees, in which stands the tasteful pagoda covering the popular Washington Spring. The halls, parlors and dining-rooms are roomy, and furnished with taste. The rooms are arranged for families, in suites, as their guests are of a class that do not wish to mingle with the general class of boarders at large hotels. The Clarendon is owned by Mr. Charles E. Leland, a younger member of the Leland family. It will accommodate five hundred guests.

Windsor Hotel (46-3, G, H).—This house was built in the spring of 1876, and opened for the first time to the public in June of that year, under the management of Mr. Charles H. Shelley. It stands on the corner of Broadway and William street, and commands a fine view of Broadway, the principal street of the village. From the roof of the house the view commands a wide range of country, embracing in its scope several villages in Saratoga county, the Hudson valley, the Green Mountains in the distant east, and the Greenfield Hills and Adirondack Mountains on the north and west, with the village of Saratoga Springs and Congress Park in immediate prospect. It is owned by Judge Hilton, and will accommodate three hundred guests.

Arlington Hotel (22-7 F).—The Arlington House has been leased for five years by new proprietors, McMichael & Denniss. The hotel is situated on the corner of Broadway and Division street, directly opposite the new United States Hotel. It is one of the best constructed hotels in Saratoga. The building is of brick, and is of modern and improved arrangement in its interior plan, having been built but a few years. It is five stories high, surmounted with a mansard roof, and presents a very neat and attractive exterior on the fashionable avenue of the town. The house fronts two of the most prominent streets of the town, and its rooms are particularly desirable, as they command views of the liveliest portions of Broadway, and the business centre of the place. It will accommodate three hundred guests.

Adelphi Hotel (19-6 F).—The Adelphi Hotel was built in the spring of 1877, and is a model modern hotel in every particular. It is centrally located on Broadway, between the two mammoth hotels, United States and Grand Union. The Adelphi has a large piazza, three stories high, fronting on Broadway, and elevated far enough above the street to command a fine view of Saratoga's most brilliant thoroughfare. The rooms are large and are very liberally furnished, and some are arranged in suites for family use, with every modern convenience.

Wm. H. McCaffrey, the proprietor, will accommodate two hundred guests.

Columbian Hotel (26-4 G).—The Columbian Hotel, Mr. C. E. Palmer, proprietor, is on Broadway, opposite Congress Park. A more beautiful and central location is not to be found in Saratoga. It is free from noise, homelike, and patronized by good society. The house is built of brick, and has a frontage of one hundred and twenty-one feet on Broadway, with a wide two-story piazza, one hundred and fifteen feet long, overlooking Congress Park and the fashionable drive of the town. The back piazza, one hundred and fifteen feet long, overlooks its own beautiful grounds and those of the Clarendon Hotel, including Washington Spring, and as one of these piazzas is always shaded, a pleasant retreat is furnished every hour of the day. All the rooms of the Columbian have pleasant outlooks, and are well furnished. It will accommodate two hundred and fifty guests.

American Hotel (21-6 F).—The American forms another of the group of hotels in the immediate vicinity of Congress and Hathorn Springs. It is at the corner of Broadway and Washington street, and is kept open all the year. It will accommodate three hundred guests.

Waverly Hotel (45-13 E).—Mr. J. H. Clay, formerly of the Everett House, has leased this commodious and popular house, where he will be happy to welcome all former patrons. At the same time he solicits the patronage of the public, feeling assured he can offer not only capacious and airy rooms, excellent beds and superior table, but all the comforts of a first-class family hotel. The house has been thoroughly refitted during the past year.

This hotel is charmingly located on North Broadway, in the midst of beautiful shade trees, and in close proximity to the famous Empire, High Rock, Red and Magnetic Springs, and only five minutes' walk from the new Woodlawn Park. It is within a few minutes' walk of Congress Park and the larger hotels, yet it offers a quiet and pleasant summer house for tourists and families. Its ample play-grounds and double piazzas, which extend entirely around the building, make it specially desirable for the latter. It will accommodate one hundred and fifty guests.

Continental Hotel (29–34 D).—This hotel is used as the Saratoga Sanitarium. (See " Medical Institutions.") It will accommodate two hundred guests.

Commercial Hotel (26–8).—The Commercial Hotel stands on the corner of Church and Matilda streets and Railroad Place. It is open all the year. It will accommodate two hundred guests.

Everett House (32–2 G).—The Everett House is situated on Broadway, a few doors south of the Clarendon Hotel, in one of the most quiet and beautiful portions of Saratoga village. Two rows of beautiful shade trees extend along either side of Broadway at this point, and afford a delightful shady retreat on the piazza of this quiet, home-like house. The proprietor, Mr. J. H. Clay, does not aim to attract much transient custom, but his guests are mainly families or persons who visit Saratoga seeking quiet, health and real comfort, and who remain some weeks at this great watering place. It will accommodate two hundred guests.

Vermont House (44–11 F).—The Vermont House, on Grove, corner of Front street, and just north of the Presbyterian church, is one of the largest and best houses in Saratoga. It is superior to some of the more pretending hotels in its handsome exterior, its well-furnished apartments, and the finish of its public rooms. The culinary department receives its supplies direct from the proprietor's farm. It will accommodate one hundred and twenty guests.

Holden House (35–7 F).—The Holden House is situated on Broadway, just north of the Arlington. The building is of brick, and has a pleasant veranda on its front, commanding a fine view of the principal street of the village. It will accommodate one hundred guests. Mr. Ramsdell, proprietor.

Franklin House (33-9 E).—The Franklin House is located on Church street, half a block from Broadway, with pleasant rooms fronting the street. It will accommodate seventy-five guests.

New York Hotel (41-10 G).—This hotel is on Church street, corner of Spring avenue, centrally located, a few blocks from the large hotels toward the south, and a few steps from the High Rock, Seltzer and other springs.

Empire Hotel (30-15 G).—The Empire Hotel is on the corner of Front street and Greenfield avenue, in the north part of the village. It is the nearest hotel to the celebrated Empire, High Rock, Saratoga Star, Seltzer and Red Springs. There is a good barn, and fine croquet-ground attached to the house. It will accommodate one hundred guests.

Albemarle Hotel (20-2 G).—The Albemarle Hotel is situated on South Broadway, three doors south of the Clarendon Hotel, in one of the most beautiful portions of Saratoga. The rooms are large, and supplied with wardrobes and clothes-presses, and the ceilings high, affording healthful and convenient apartments. Congress, Columbian, Washington and Hathorn Springs are within two blocks, and the beautful Congress Park and the prominent hotels within one block of the house. Its central location, excellent table, well-furnished and spacious rooms, make this house one to be much desired as a home while at the springs. It will accommodate fifty guests.

Mansion House (39-6 G).—The Mansion House is situated on Spring avenue, within a few rods of Excelsior and Union Springs. It is in the midst of the beautiful Excelsior Park, and is surrounded by a large and handsome lawn, well covered with tall forest trees. Many of the most refined and wealthy families of our great cities spend the summer months here, attracted by its proximity to the Excelsior, Union and White Sulphur Springs, the beauty of its surroundings, and the superior style in which the house is kept. Within the park are several cottages, and families occupying them and wishing to avoid the annoyance of cooks and cooking, can obtain their meals at the Mansion House. R. S. Moscrip, proprietor, will accommodate fifty guests.

Mount Pleasant Hotel (47-2 G).—This hotel is located on

Broadway, nearly opposite the Windsor Hotel, a few steps from Congress Park. C. H. Teft, proprietor, will accommodate fifty guests.

Central Hotel (24-8 E).—The Central Hotel is just one block from the railroad depot on Church street. It has a roomy piazza.

Germania Hotel (36-7 F).—The Germania is opposite the United States Hotel, on Broadway. The location of this house is the very centre of the village. It has an excellent view of the avenue, and of the arrival and departure of guests, as it is opposite Division street, which leads to the depot.

Spencer House (42-7 E).—The Spencer House has an entrance on Railroad Place, opposite the depot, on Matilda street. This house is very conveniently located, as the rear faces the depot but two doors from the United States Hotel. It will accommodate one hundred guests.

Centennial House (7 E).—This house is located on Matilda street, two doors north of the United States Hotel, with the depot in the rear. It is within the group of the great Saratoga hotels. Mrs. James Carroll, proprietress, will accommodate fifty guests.

BOARDING-HOUSES.

The problem of providing accommodations for the fifteen or twenty thousand people who inhabit Saratoga during the summer months, is one that has annually perplexed the experienced caterers of the great watering place. The hotel capacity does not exceed nine or ten thousand, yet the number of the visiting population in July and August is certainly fifteen thousand. There are, however, numerous boarding-houses scattered throughout the village. Some of these afford excellent accommodation at moderate prices, and are decidedly home-like and healthful. We advise those who visit Saratoga seeking health as well as pleasure, to look for board at some of these good boarding-houses, where they can find the comfort of a quiet home at very moderate prices. Many of these houses have beautiful lawns for croquet and other out-door sports, and are under competent management.

Temple Grove Seminary (100-8 J).—This excellent institution is situated in the eastern part of the village, on what was formerly known as Temple Hill, and in the midst of Temple Grove. The grounds occupy the whole square on Spring street, between Circular and Regent streets. It is under the efficient management of Prof. Chas. F. Dowd, a graduate of Yale College, and affords fine advantages for a complete and solid education. During the long vacation from June to September, the building is opened as a summer resort. It will accommodate two hundred guests.

Dr. Strong (78-9 J).—Dr. Strong (see "Medical Institutions,") will accommodate two hundred guests.

Broadway Hall (72-13 E).—This celebrated boarding-house is beautifully located a little up Broadway, and on higher ground than any other boarding-house in the place, and consequently is airy and healthy. It is surrounded by a lawn of about an acre, and in the midst of magnificent shade trees, on one of the finest avenues in this country, and is within ten minutes' walk of all the principal springs. No other house in town has as great a proportion of high, large, well-ventilated and pleasant rooms. The proprietor, Mr. J. Howland, is one of Saratoga's most respected citizens, and has had several years' experience in his business, and spares no effort to make the Broadway worthy of the liberal patronage which it receives from the best class of people. It will accommodate one hundred guests.

Washington Hall is on Broadway, opposite the Waverly Hotel, with splendid grounds for croquet, surrounded by shady trees, a few steps from the great hotel group. J. Starr, proprietor, will accommodate one hundred guests.

Wilber House (4 C).—The Wilber House is located on Washton street, just above the railroad track. It has excellent garden plots. This house is intended as a pleasant home for families. L. P. Sawyer, proprietor, will accommodate one hundred guests.

Elmwood Hall (58-11 G).—This house is located on Front street, nearly opposite the Town Hall Square, and directly opposite the Vermont House. It is near the spring group—High Rock, Seltzer, Red, &c.—and but a few blocks from the hotel group. R. R. Tennant, proprietor, will accommodate eighty guests.

Morey House (62-4 C).—The Morey House is on Franklin

street. It is situated but a short distance from the principal springs
and the leading hotels in the place, and only a few steps from the
railroad dépot near the head of the street. Franklin street, on
which it stands, is one of the most beautifully shaded streets of this
charming village, and the furnishing and appointments of this house
are in full harmony with its clean and attractive surroundings. N.
D. Morey, proprietor, will accommodate eighty guests.

Pierpont Hotel (6 G).—This charming retreat, located at
the corner of Regent and White streets, near Union avenue, the
most elevated portion of Saratoga, is five minutes' leisurely walk to
Congress Springs, and commands a fine view of the park and principal drives to the racecourse and lake. Mrs. J. B. Reed, proprietress, will accommodate eighty guests.

Pitney House (64-2 B).—The Pitney House is on Congress
street, and is kept by Mr. J. Pitney, who has a large farm, from
which he supplies the table with fruit, vegetables, milk and cream,
fresh from the farm twice a day. The Pitney thus has a very great
advantage over other houses, which depend upon the supplies in the
village markets. Many of the guests are old patrons who have
boarded at this house every season for years, and who appreciate
the luxuries which this house places before its guests at the table.
Two neat cottages on the grounds adjoining the house, are rented to
such as desire more seclusion than the large house affords.

Thorn House (68-9 J).—The Thorn House is on Phila street,
corner of Circular, Circular street being the most fashionable street
in the village for private summer residents, and a few blocks from
the great hotel group. C. A. Thorn, proprietor, will accommodate
forty-five guests.

Dr. Robert Hamilton (4 C).—Dr. Hamilton, (see "Medical
Institutions,") will accommodate thirty guests.

Huestis House (59-2 G).—The Huestis House is on Broadway, two doors south of the Windsor Hotel. Its location is very
desirable, as it commands an elegant view of Broadway and is but a
step from Congress Park and Spring. J. L. Huestis, proprietor,
will accommodate sixty guests.

Circular Street House (54-10 I).—This house is located on
Circular street, near Phila, commanding an elegant view of this

avenue, with beautiful garden plots.   John Palmer, proprietor,
will accommodate fifty guests.

Albion House (48–12 G).—The Albion House is located on
Front street, near the spring group—Seltzer, High Rock, Star and
Empire.   O. Magee, proprietor, will accommodate fifty guests.

Osborn House (13 G).—The Osborn is located at Front and
Van Dam streets, nearly opposite the bottling-house of the Seltzer
Spring, and therefore convenient to the spring group.   It is but ten
minutes' walk from the great hotel group.   Mrs. Ellis, proprietress,
will accommodate fifty guests.

Balch House (49–10 F).—The Balch House is located on
Broadway between the town hall and the Presbyterian church.   It
has elegant rooms and garden plots, and also croquet grounds.   This
boarding-house is strictly first-class, and its location makes it
specially desirable for families.   Mrs. Balch, proprietress, will accommodate thirty guests.

Dr. Haines (7 K).—Dr. Haines, (see "Medical Institutions,")
will accommodate twenty-five guests.

WALKS AND AMUSEMENTS.

There are a number of walks in and about Saratoga Springs, and
the visitor will find ample space for exercise and amusement.   Shady
woods, breezy hills, and crowded streets brilliant with carriages,
mingle in charming confusion, and present varied attractions in
every direction.

To give plain directions to enable the visitor to dispense with a
guide, we will use the great hotels as a starting point from which to
make such walking or riding tours as seem desirable.   Of course,
the grand promenade is Broadway.   Here one may see the great
hotels, the carriages and the gorgeous apparel.   The broad road,
kept in fine order, and the wide, grass-trimmed sidewalks, are
crowded with teams and people, and the scene is at once animated,
high-colored and interesting.   Mingling in the multitude on the
walk, we may turn to the north.   Stores fully equal to city shops
line the way.   The American and the great United States Hotels

soon come opposite. Next stand the Arlington Hotel and the Holden House. The street turns slightly, and, after passing the town hall, the hotels change to private houses and the stores to gardens. Crossing the railroad, the Waverly House is passed on the right, and the Washington House and Broadway Hall on the left. Keeping on up the gentle hill, a number of new and very pretty gardens and villas are met, and between the houses on the right open wide views over the open country. The hills beyond rise into lovely mountain ranges on the horizon. These are the Green Mountains, in Vermont, and in many places about the springs they make an ever-beautiful framework to the landscape. This part of the town is laid out with new streets, and in time will become a fashionable and desirable quarter. Many new houses have been put up, and the rows of young trees and well-made streets will soon attract a desirable population. Broadway continues on some distance further into the country, and eventually leads to Glen Mitchell, about two and a half miles from the great hotels. Of this place, more when we come to speak of drives. The return walk leads again into all the crowds of elegant loiterers about the grand hotels, and ends where it began.

Another and shorter walk turns to the south from the great hotels, and follows South Broadway. Congress Park is on the left, and the site of the Grand Hotel, burned October 1st, 1874, and Crystal Spring by the Columbian Hotel, and the hotel itself, are on the right. The Clarendon comes next, with Washington Spring in its court. This is a most delightful place, and is patronized by the select and wealthy few who prefer to take their comfort without so much grandeur as the larger houses bestow. On the corner of William street opposite the Clarendon, is the Roman Catholic church, on the southeast corner stands the Windsor Hotel, and south of these are the Albemarle and Everett Houses. Just beyond the Everett House, Ballston avenue turns off diagonally to the right. From this point we can turn either way and wander through quiet streets, lined with beautiful and costly houses, each half-buried in its shrubbery and gardens. By turning to the left we enter Circular street, and may pass quite around Congress Park, and so back to the hotels through East Congress street. Congress Spring and

Columbian Spring are both in this fine park, and if you care to enter you may wander at will.

The Late John Morrissey.—Starting out from the great hotels, we may, in a little longer walk, see some of the minor wonders of the place. Turning to the left, down East Congress street, past Congress Spring and Park, we come to the opening of the broad Union avenue that leads to the racecourse and the lake. Just opposite the park is a large brick building, formerly owned and occupied by the late John Morrissey, for purposes best known to himself and his patrons. It is still involved in the mysteries of "ways that are dark and tricks that are vain."

Indian Encampments (5-7 H, I).—In the grove on top of the hill to the left is a collection of promiscuous amusements for the children and somewhat frisky adult population. Archery, hobby-horse, whirligigs, tenpins, ice cream, lemonade, &c., form some of the enticements of this fascinating play-ground. By turning to the right, and passing along Circular street around Congress Park and toward the Geyser Spring, we come to the Indian camp. A number of shanties, half tent, half hut, are planted here, and a gypsy band, part Canadian, part Indian, live therein, and sell such things as good Indians are supposed to wear and use. Small boys urge the visitor to set up the persuasive cent, that they may hit it with their little arrows, and pocket the same. The performance is varied by sundry domestic scenes, with appropriate dresses and motions, and the whole affair is very picturesque, and is highly instructive to the inquiring mind. To be sure, it is a little theatrical, and one has grave doubts concerning the fidelity of the display to nature, but it serves to fill an idle hour, and amuse children and others.

Circular Railway.—This railway is a small piece of track built in a circle, and provided with small cars. Here one may have the infantile joy of a ride in an enlarged baby-carriage, round and round.

The Springs.—Here the gay scenes peculiar to Saratoga begin. Hundreds of people are gathered around the fountains, sipping or drinking deep as their fancy or doctors bid, and the road is crowded with carriages bringing their festive loads to the waters. There is much of wealth and display, good nature and fashion, flirtation and fine clothes, and it is altogether amusing and jolly. First comes the old Red Spring, with its box of a bottling-house. Opposite, near the railroad, is the Saratoga "A" Spring, and beyond to the left is the Empire Spring. The Star, High Rock and Seltzer offer their varied charms next in order. It is true, the scene is not wholly lovely. There are a number of rather disagreeable old traps on the bluff and along the wretched little street, but one may easily drown such minor griefs in a tumbler of salt water. We escape up the long step by High Rock, and soon reach Broadway and the hotels again. Saratoga Springs has its objections, its old shanties, and offensive advertisements painted on its rocks and fences, its muddy brook and ill-kept lanes ; but we can easily forgive them all on reaching Broadway and its palaces.

Another shorter walk past the railroad station, and then to the right, through Clinton street, and on out into the open country, will give one a good idea of the newer portions of the village, and afford a charming view of the country to the north and west. On reaching the hill, just clear of the village, a wide view will be obtained of the Kayaderosseras Mountains in the northwest, and the blue peaks of the Catskills at the far south. Returning, we may keep off to the left, and strike Broadway just beyond the Waverly House.

Other walks may be taken at will through the village, with no fear of losing the way, as the tall roofs and towers of the great hotels readily serve as guide-marks in every direction.

The Horse Races.—The horse races take place at the magnificent new racecourse on Union avenue, in July and August. They are usually arranged in two meeting, the first extending from about July 20th to August 5th, and the second from about August 10th to August 21st. There are five or six racing-days in each meeting, and great interest is always manifested in them. The meetings are under the charge of the Saratoga Association, and everything is done to render the races agreeable and acceptable to the tens of thousands who witness them. The trots occur at Glen Mitchell, usually on alternate days with the running races at the racecourse.

Base-ball Matches.—Base-ball matches and foot-races are held every season, at Glen Mitchell, between the various colleges and other organizations.   Military regiments also camp here every summer, and add new life and interest to the place.

Boat Races.—Rowing regattas are held at Saratoga annually, and embrace races between college crews and other amateurs as well as professional oarsmen.   These usually begin in July, and occur at intervals during the season.

Saratoga Bazaar.—The Bazaar is situated next to Hathorn Spring, both having the same entrance.   It is tastefully arranged in different booths or stalls, where merchants can offer their wares, which are numerous and attractive.   The gorgeous array of different kinds of goods make a beautiful appearance, and reminds one of a large church fair.   It is well worthy of a visit, and a pleasant stroll through the various aisles affords the visitor amusement as well as an opportunity of purchasing articles of vertu, *bric-a-brac*, notions, etc.   The Bazaar is under the management of Mr. Myers.

Congress Park.—This beautiful park comprises almost the entire plot of ground encompassed by Broadway, Congress and Circular streets.   Originally a forest, possessing many natural attractions, it has been materially improved by grading, draining and the addition of many architectural adornments, until it now presents a most beautiful appearance, and is one of Saratoga's principal charms.   During the year 1876, the Congress and Empire Spring Company expended nearly $100,000 on these improvements, and now it surpasses all other parks of equal size in the United States in the beauty of its graceful and artistic architecture.   The grade of the low ground was raised from two to seven feet, and a new plan of drainage adopted, which involved in its system the elegant new reservoir and the charming miniature lake.   The grand entrance is at the junction of Congress street and Broadway, near the Grand Union Hotel and Congress Hall, on what is now called Monument Square.   On entering, turn to the right, and you may pass through a short colonnade to the graceful spring-house over the Columbian Spring, or from the entrance turn to the left through a longer colonnade, and you come to the interior of the artistic pavilion over Congress Spring.   In this interior the Congress Spring water is passed by uniformed attendants, and you may partake while seated at a little table upon which the water will be served.   The process of drawing the water is novel, and you will be interested to observe it, while the mode of serving affords opportunity to drink at leisure and at ease, without the jostling and spilling incident to the old systems pursued at the other springs in town. Passing down a few steps and along the colonnade, you reach the elegant *café*, where hot coffee and other refreshments may be obtained and may be partaken of while listening to the park music and enjoying the charming view of the lakes and grounds from the *café* pavilion. Passing from the *café*, you may stroll at will, visiting the lakes and the shaded lawns, and listening to the delightful music of the very celebrated Park Band, which plays morning, afternoon and evening. In the evening the band occupies the very unique and artistic music pavilion in the centre of the lake. Strolling along to the south part of the grounds, you may visit the deer shelter and park, where are several animals that roam and skip about within the enclosure, greatly to the delight of the children and the amusement of the adults. In the park, amid the flowers and shrubs, strolling over the grass-covered, shaded lawns, or lounging under the grand old forest trees, enchanted by the charming music—here it is that one may enjoy the supreme delights of a genuine rural summer resort. Every convenience for park enjoyment is here afforded, including abundant settees and shade, and the security of efficient police supervision. The grounds are thoroughly lighted by gas at night, rendering them available as a place of evening resort. The scene in the evening, on the occasion of one of the grand concerts, is remarkably brilliant and charmingly fascinating.

Admission to the park is regulated by tickets, for which a nominal charge is made. Single admission tickets, admitting to all except evening concerts, 10 cents each, or twenty-five tickets for $2, fifty for $3.50, one hundred for $5. No charge for children under ten years of age accompanied by older persons. Admission to grand and sacred evening concert, 25 cents, unless advertised otherwise. Tickets may be obtained at the entrance to the park.

Some may wonder that in a resort like Saratoga there is no park open to the public without charge, but such is the fact. Congress Park, however, supplies for this trifling charge, the desirable seclusion and security of a private park.

Access may be obtained to Congress or Columbian Spring without entering the park, and the waters at all approaches to the springs are served free of charge. To reach the free entrance to Congress Spring, pass along Congress street from Broadway and the spring will be observed a few yards east of the park entrance. Free access to the Columbian Spring may be obtained on Broadway nearly opposite the Columbian Hotel, and a few steps south of the park entrance.

Excelsior Park.—This park comprises a number of acres of land extending from Lake avenue to Excelsior Lake, and including the grove. The land about the spring and the lake is laid out in house lots, and some have already been sold and built upon. The spring is well worth a visit, as the system of preparing the water for export is somewhat peculiar to the place. Visitors are freely shown all the processes, and allowed to roam at will through the grounds of the park. Leaving the spring, we can return by the way of the path through the woods, or take a little longer route back by the way of Spring avenue. Directly before the spring-house is a road leading to the White Sulphur and Eureka Springs. Near the road is a small brook called Loughberry creek, and the Minnehaha Spring. The large house on the top of the western slope of the valley is the Mansion House. Here a road leads north, around Excelsior Lake, but we follow Spring avenue to the left, and soon reach the Loughberry Water Works, where the great Holly engines continually pump the lake-water through the village. A few moments may be well spent here examining these splendid engines in motion.

Geyser Park.—Start from the great hotels, follow Broadway south to Ballston avenue, which branches off from Broadway in the south part of the village, to the southwest. Follow this avenue under its shady trees until it crosses the Rensselaer and Saratoga Railroad, when the large bottling-house of Geyser Spring will be distinctly seen across the lake to the right.

DRIVES.

The beautiful scenery of Saratoga affords the visitor many pleasant drives to the numerous points of interest in the vicinity. Among the most enjoyable of these is the drive to the

Spouting Springs.—The best time to go is the latter part of the afternoon, as the Champion Spring gives its regular performance at five o'clock every day except Sunday. Follow South Broadway to the third turn to the right, and enter Ballston avenue. This street leads to the southwest, diagonally from Broadway, and cannot be mistaken. After escaping from the houses, the road passes a small grove, and another Indian encampment, where the domestic squaw and infantile papoose display as much of picturesque beauty as they can command, or sell such trinkets as their arts can make. Greater charms entice us on—the glass-works and the great natural soda-fountain. The open fields that follow give a wide outlook over the country, and to the mountains on either side. Yonder black pile of buildings to the right, and just beyond the railroad, are the glass-works of the Congress and Empire Spring Company. If one has time it is well worth the while to turn aside here and look in upon the swarthy workers, dipping their long iron tubes into the white heat of the furnace, and drawing out the viscid mass that, with dextrous toil and distended cheeks, they blow into bottles of different sizes.

Another grove invites us to walk along its shady edge, and splendid views of the Green Mountains open on the left, and then we come to the new village that has sprung up about the strange group of springs that have been here discovered. A number of rather startling signs point the way to the various springs, and, crossing the track, we find them all within a few rods of each other. At the top of the hill, near the railroad, stands the Triton House. This summer hotel is most delightfully located, overlooking the two ponds, the waterfall and the various springs. A depot is to be erected here, and the village made a regular stopping-place on the road; and, as the springs and the neighborhood are both attractive, the hotel will no doubt be liberally patronized.

The Triton Spring is in a small building just beyond the Triton House, and near Geyser Lake. This sheet of water, on the right-hand side of the road, is opened freely to such as care to row about its placid waters, among the little islands and shaded nooks that make the lake pretty and attractive. A sign informs the passing world of this privilege, with a caution to the voyager not to "abuse it." From the lake we pass on towards the Vichy Spring. This is a spouting spring, poetically set in an iron fountain under a wooden canopy, on the west side of Geyser Lake, and just north of Ballston avenue. There is a pretty lawn with a number of trees, and a picturesque farm-house on one side and the placid little lake on the other, so that the surroundings are quite beautiful and attractive.

The Geyser Spring stands directly opposite the lake, and a few rods from the road. It is in a large brick building below the falls, and the drive-way leads directly to the door. The grounds are neatly laid out, and the beautiful waterfall, and the rapid stream with its grassy and shaded banks, dashing past the bottling-house, combine to give the spring very picturesque surroundings. In the centre of the room is a well about six feet square, and from the bottom rises an iron pipe, from which leaps the creamy water of the spring. To allow it full play, there is an opening in the ceiling, and here it rises and falls, day and night, continually. At one side a faucet, with a nose like a soda-fountain, enables one to draw a glass. The water boils and bubbles out, mingled with bubbles of gas precisely like cream soda. When the bubbles have escaped, the water has a wonderful pearly purity that tempts one to drink bountifully. A glass globe on the well-curb has a stream of water flowing through it and escaping at the top. This enables us to see the thick stream of bubbling gas as it rises through the water and makes an extremely pretty display. A large business is here carried on in bottling this valuable and delicious water, and visitors are politely shown all the processes in detail.

Leaving the spring-house by the rear door, we enter the delightful landscape scenery around the spring, and follow a path down into the little dell where the stream flows on towards the ravine. From the rustic bridge over the brook is a good view of the waterfall, and near it may be found a natural sulphur spring. Crossing the railroad embankment by a foot-path, we enter the romantic valley where stands the Champion. This remarkable spring is not protected by any building, and its waters fall on the bare ground, mingle with some fresh water springs, and flow away into the brook beyond There is a small bottling-house near by, and an old mill. These buildings are not permanent. The water for drinking and bottling is drawn in the bottling-house. It is a limpid, cold and delightful drink, and every one should have at least a taste, fresh from the lower deeps of the earth. The hour has come for the usual daily performance, and the place is crowded with carriages and pleasure parties, gathered to see the display. Two men come out and take off the cap on the top of the upright iron pipe. At once the water leaps in a pure white column a hundred feet into the air, and falls in showers of glistening spray, presenting a brilliant spectacle of hydraulics, the like of which is not to be seen this side of the great Geysers of Iceland.

Ballston Spa is the county town of Saratoga county, and is seven miles south of Saratoga Springs. The drive is through Ballston avenue, past Geyser Spring, following by the side of the railroad to Ballston village. It is a very pretty town of about four thousand inhabitants, with beautifully-shaded streets and several objects of interest to the tourist.

The village has long been celebrated for its mineral springs. The waters are quite similar in chemical properties to those of Saratoga, and are doubtless drawn from the same natural medicinal reservoir. The principal springs already developed are the Ballston Artesian Lithia, Washington, Franklin, Sans Souci and the new Corporation Spring. The Ballston Artesian Lithia Spring is the most celebrated, and its bottling-house is on the Saratoga drive, at the north end of the village.

Lake Lonely.—This small lake is not far from the village of Saratoga, and near Union avenue. It is rather pretty, and has a good echo on the eastern shore, but beyond this it has no special interest.

Chapman's Hill.—This makes a pleasant drive, and the view from the top is said to be very good.

Wagman's Hill is higher and more distant, giving still more extended and striking views. A number of mineral springs are here shown, one of which, charged with an inflammable gas, is very interesting.

Wearing Hill.—This is on the Mount Pleasant road, and makes a good all-day excursion. The ride is about fifteen miles, through a pleasant country, and the view from the top includes Ballston,

Saratoga, Schenectady, Waterford, Mechanicsville, Schuylerville, and Saratoga and Round Lakes.

The Prospect Hills of Greenfield.—These hills are about three and a half miles northwest of Saratoga Springs. They are reached by the way of Waring avenue west to Granger's Four Corners, thence north two miles; or through Greenfield avenue in a northwesterly direction to Locust Grove Corners, thence north half a mile. The view of the Green Mountains is very fine, and, to the south, the Helderberg Hills of Albany and the Catskills beyond, fringe the horizon.

Corinth.—Here are some bold falls on the upper Hudson. The carriage ride is fifteen miles. By the Adirondack Railway, the falls are reached from a station called Jessup's Landing.

Luzerne.—This pretty village, at the confluence of the Scandaga and Hudson, is about twenty miles from the springs. It may be reached by road, or the Adirondack Railroad. Lake Luzerne is a popular resort for boating and fishing, and is provided with two good hotels.

Saratoga Lake.—Turn down East Congress street, past Congress Park, and enter the broad avenue leading to the east. This is Union avenue, the great fashionable drive. In about a mile the village is cleared, and we pass the new race track on the right. The old track, now used for a training-ground, is opposite. At the new track races take place in July and August, attracting immense throngs of visitors from all parts of the country. Even if no races are going on, it is worth while to drive into the grounds and see the place. Beyond the racecourse, the road leads down hill, and affords some lovely views of the Green Mountains. After passing a mile or two of the meadows and woods, the road climbs out on top of a level plateau, and reaches Moon's Lake House. This house is situated on a grassy bluff, about fifty feet above the lake, affording a full view of its placid waters. Saratoga Lake, about eight miles long and perhaps two miles wide, is one of the most beautiful sheets of water to be found. The wooded hills at the end, and the glimpses of the Catskills beyond, the farms and meadows on either bank, the little steamers and pleasure boats everywhere busy on the water, and the elegant grounds adjoining the house, make this a favorite place of resort. Black bass and pickerel abound in the water, and at Mr. Moon's tables, out of doors or on his piazzas, we may have fish fresh from the water and fried potatoes that have become famous throughout the Union. The park-like establishment next to the hotel is the property of the late Frank Leslie, the New York publisher, and it is well worth a visit. The boat-races held here in the summer attract a great company every season, and make a feature of Saratoga life. Myers' Hotel is another resort on the eastern shore of the lake, and is reached by turning to the left just before reachin Moon's house. On the ride back to the village, some fine mountain views may be noticed soon after leaving the lake.

Gridley's Trout Ponds.—A shorter drive in the same direction may be taken to a picturesque little dell near the racecourse, where a series of fish-ponds afford sport for fish-lovers. Mr. Gridley, the proprietor, raises brook trout in great quantities, and during the season opens his ponds to such as care to fish, and are willing to pay a dollar a pound for all they capture and take away. The fish are kept till three years old, and are then in fine order for the table. The visitors are provided with lines and bait, and chairs if they wish them, and under the shade of the trees they may pick out as much speckled liveliness as they want. As there are many thousand fish in the ponds, the sport is both active and abundant. To reach the ponds, drive out over Union avenue to the third turn on the right beyond Congress Park. Turn here, and follow the road till a large brick house is reached. Just here, a lane on the left will lead directly to the ponds. Half a hundred carriages often gather around these ponds on a pleasant summer's day, while their occupants go a-fishing in royal style.

EXCURSIONS.

No. 1. To Jessup's Landing, on the Hudson river, seventeen miles from Saratoga, via Adirondack Railroad, at the edge of the wild and mountainous Adirondack region. The objects of interest are the seventy-feet falls in the Hudson, with the half-mile rapids above ; the grand and beautiful mountain scenery, and the extensive manufactory of the Hudson River Pulp Company for making pulp

E

from wood, for the manufacture of paper. Dine at the hotel, and return to Saratoga by the afternoon train.

No. 2. To Luzerne, Warren county, N. Y., twenty-two miles from Saratoga, via Adirondack Railroad. Leave Saratoga on the morning train, crossing the Sacondaga river on the railroad bridge, four hundred and fifty feet long and ninety-six feet high. Visit the charming little village on the banks of the Hudson river, between the mountains on either side six hundred feet high; the rapids and falls in the river; the beautiful Lake Luzerne, affording fine trout-fishing or sailing. Dine at Butler's or Rockwell's Hotel, and return in the afternoon of the same day, or the next day, as you choose, to Saratoga.

No. 3. To Schroon Lake, Warren county N. Y., via Adirondack Railroad, fifty miles, to Riverside, on the Hudson, thence by stage six miles to Pottersville, foot of Schroon Lake. Steamboat excursion on the lake; Leland's or Windsor Hotel; Schroon Lake village; fine fishing or hunting; charmingly picturesque scenery. Remain over night at any of the hotels. Return via same route to Saratoga next day or later.

No. 4. To Blue Mt. Lake and Cedar River Falls, Hamilton county, N. Y., via morning train on Adirondack Railroad, to North Creek, fifty-eight miles; thence by stage, twenty miles, to Riley's, formerly Jackson's, via "Fourteenth Indian River;" thence to Blue Mt. Lake, ten miles from Jackson's, at evening of same day. Two or three good hotels and boarding-houses in vicinity of Racquette Lake; Moose Lake; Mohican Lake; Three Cedar Lakes; Sumner Lake; Shedd Lake; Moose River, the finest trout-fishing in the Adirondacks. The route to Cedar River Falls diverges from Jackson's via stage to Wakley's Hotel, Cedar River Falls, twelve miles distant. Return at leisure via same route.

No. 5. To Lake George, by morning train on Delaware and Hudson Canal Company's railroad to Whitehall, Ticonderoga and Baldwin's; thence by steamer on Lake George to Fort William Henry Hotel; thence by stage to Glen Falls; thence by rail to Fort Edward and Saratoga same day. This is the most delightful excursion that can be completed in one day from Saratoga.

Or, via morning train on Delaware and Hudson Canal Company's railroad to Fort Edward, Glen Falls; thence by stage through wild and mountainous scenery to Lake George. Arrive at Fort William Henry Hotel for dinner, remain over night, and next morning at nine o'clock take steamer down Lake George to Baldwin's; thence by Delaware and Hudson Canal Company's railroad to Ticonderoga, Whitehall and Saratoga, arriving in time for supper.

No. 6. To Ballston Spa, seven miles, via Delaware and Hudson Canal Company's railroad, or by carriage. Visit the Artesian Lithia Spring, Sans Souci Boiling Spring, and others. Return at 3 or 6 P. M., on same day.

No. 7. To Round Lake, via Delaware and Hudson Canal Company's railroad, twelve miles. National Camp Meeting Grounds of Methodist Church. Return same day at 3 or 6 P. M.

No. 8. To Union College, Schenectady, N. Y., twenty-two miles, via morning train Delaware and Hudson Canal Company's railroad, to Schenectady. Visit the college and city. Return by five o'clock train, same day, to Saratoga, by same route.

No. 9. To Hoosac Tunnel, Mass., via morning train on Delaware and Hudson Canal Company's railroad, to Troy ; thence, via Troy and Boston Railroad, to Hoosac Tunnel, seven miles long Remain over night at Ballou House. Return to Saratoga next day, by same route.

No. 10. To Saratoga Battle Grounds, fifteen miles east of Saratoga Springs, by private carriage or stage, to Bemis' Heights and Stillwater. Dine at Schuylerville, and return same day or next day, as you choose.

No. 11. To Manchester, Vt., via Renssalaer and Saratoga Railroad, to Rutland, on morning train; thence, via Harlem Extension Railroad, to Manchester, Vt. Remain over night at Equinox House, and return next day by same route or via North Bennington and Troy.

There are many other excursions of shorter length, which we have described under the head of "Drives." These will be found pleasant and healthful. The longer ones are limitless in number and extent Our aim is to suggest those more easily accomplished, and which naturally belong to Saratoga as a rendezvous.

Dr. Strong's Remedial Institute, Saratoga Springs, N. Y.

Popular Summer Resort. Also, Open all the Year.

It is beautifully located in close proximity to the principal Springs, Hotels and Park, with ample grounds, elegant and complete in all appointments. It is the resort of leading men in Church and State, for rest and recreation, as well as treatment. Among its patrons are Dr. T. L. Cuyler; Ex-Govs. Wells and Boardman ; Bishops Simpson, Robinson, Harris, Haven, Foster, &c. ; College Presidents Haven, Foss, Chadburne, Tuttle, Payne, Park, &c. ; Medical Professors Armor, Ross and Knapp, and others equally well known. The parlor is furnished with an organ and Steinway Parlor-Grand Piano for the benefit of guests. The house is free from the objectionable feature of invalidism, and abounds in means of amusement. The boarding department is of the highest order, and is of the nature of a family hotel.

Patients from the South and warmer climates, who have spent the winter here, give decided preference to this climate.   There is scarcely any disease but may be benefited, more or less, by some one of the Cathartic, Diuretic, Alterative, Alkaline, or Tonic Spring Waters, which are equally efficient in winter as in summer.

The proprietors are graduates of the Medical Department of N. Y. University. The Institute is furnished with every comfort and appliance for the treatment of Nervous, Lung, Female and Chronic Diseases. Among the agents employed are TURKISH, RUSSIAN, ROMAN, SULPHUR AND ELECTRO-THERMAL BATHS, SWEDISH MOVEMENT CURE, OXYGEN AND MEDICATED INHALATIONS, COMPRESSED AND RARIFIED AIR, GALVANIC AND FARADIC ELECTRICITY, CALISTHENICS, &c. SEND FOR CIRCULAR.

H. VOULLIEME,

Manufacturer of Rich and Choice Confections,

ICE CREAM, SODA WATER AND FRUIT ICES.

CONGRESS PARK CARAMELS A SPECIALTY.

GENERAL DEPOT FOR VOULLIEME'S CONGRESS PARK CARAMELS.

Also, Importer of Precious Stones and Jewelry, Onyx, Cameo, Amethyst, Blood Stone, Smoked Topaz, Calcedony. Amber, Lapis Lazuli, Agate, Cornelian, Malachite, etc. Splendid specimens in the rough state.

No. 361 Broadway, Saratoga Springs, N. Y.

UNDER ADELPHI HOTEL.

☞ Goods shipped to any part of the United States and Canada.

PEOPLE'S EVENING LINE
BETWEEN
NEW YORK AND ALBANY.

DURING THE SEASON OF NAVIGATION
THE MAGNIFICENT STEAMERS of THIS LINE WILL
LEAVE NEW YORK
Every Week-day at 6 P. M., from Pier 41. North River, as follows

DREW,   ST. JOHN
Capt. S. J. ROE,   Capt. THOS. POST,

Monday, Wednesday, Friday.   **Tuesday, Thursday, Saturday.**

Arriving in Albany in time to connect with morning trains NORTH. EAST and WEST.

LEAVE ALBANY
Every Week-day at 8 P. M., from Steamboat Landing:

ST. JOHN   DREW,
Monday, Wednesday, Friday. | **Tuesday, Thursday, Saturday.**

Connecting at New York with ALL EARLY TRAINS for the SOUTH and EAST. Meals on the European Plan.

BAGGAGE TRANSFERRED FREE Between New York Central Depot and Steamers at Albany. Baggage Checked to Destination.

FOR TICKETS IN NEW YORK,

Apply at the Company's Ticket Office on the wharf (Pier 41, North River); at New York Transfer Co. Offices, 944 and 1323 Broadway—736 Sixth Avenue—4 Court Street Brooklyn, and at all principal Hotels and Ticket Offices in New York and on board the Steamers.

W. W. EVERETT,	J. C. HEWITT,	M. B. WATERS,
President.	*Gen. T. Agt.*	*Gen. Pass. Agt*

CONGRESS WATER.

Cathartic and Alterative. Is a well-known specific for **Constipation, Indigestion,** and all disorders of the **Stomach, Liver and Kidneys.**

Ninety years' popular use attests its purity, safety and superiority to all waters of this class. Avoid all coarse, **irritating waters, foreign or domestic**; they impair the digestive organs and kidneys, thereby **inducing** irreparable results.

None Genuine Sold on Draught.

Address, **CONGRESS AND EMPIRE SPRINGS CO.,**
SARATOGA SPRINGS, NEW YORK.

MEREDITH CLYMER, M. D.,
Late Professor of Practice of Medicine in the University of New York, etc.

PROF. CLYMER, writing on *Lithœmia* (Acid Dyspepsia), says:

"Of the different natural Alkaline Mineral Waters named no one fulfills as well so many of the required indications in the treatment of this chronic disorder as the water of the Congress Spring, at Saratoga. Whilst other waters containing many of the salts found in this may, sometimes, be used in like cases temporarily without harm, their prolonged use is sure to be attended with unpleasant effects, even in young persons, and those otherwise with sound organs, on account of their *harshness;* but in persons where degenerative changes already exist in the kidneys and other organs, and in old persons, where such changes are constantly present, I have repeatedly known most *disastrous consequences* follow the use of the *stronger* and *harsh* waters, both native and imported, when taken in full doses and for any length of time. In an experience of over forty years with the Congress Spring Water, (and which to-day is as perfect in its chemical constitution and in its remedial properties as at any previous time,) I have not known a single instance where, when used in suitable cases, any unpleasant effects followed its habitual use at any age. This harmlessness, as well as its efficiency, may, I think, be rightly attributed to the happy proportions in which the various alkaline salts which enter into its composition, and which are so potent for good in this class of disorders, are combined, and which in their treatment makes Congress Water *facile princeps* amongst the natural mineral waters.

"It is not alone as a Cathartic and Laxative that the Congress Spring Water is of great worth in the management of these affections (and as such its action is mild and prompt), but it is when used continuously and in less quantity that we derive so much benefit, without risk to the patient, as an alterative and regulator of the digestive functions."

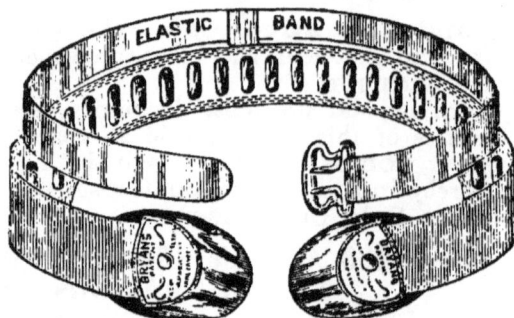